BELIEF
IN THE NEW TESTAMENT

Rudolf Schnackenburg

Translated by
Jeremy Moiser

PAULIST PRESS
Deus Books
New York, N.Y.   Paramus, N.J.

Originally published as *Glaubensimpulse aus dem Neuen Testament* by Patmos-Verlag, Düsseldorf, 1973. Published in England as *The Will to Believe* by Darton, Longman and Todd Ltd., 1974.

Cover by Dan Pezza

Library of Congress
Card Catalog No. 74-14023

ISBN 0-8091-1847-5

Published by Paulist Press
Editorial Office: 1865 Broadway, N.Y., N.Y. 10023
Business Office: 400 Sette Drive, Paramus, N.J. 07652

Printed and bound in the
United States of America

Contents

vi

Translator's Preface

In the interests of uniformity, I thought it advisable to use one English version of the Bible throughout the book, and the Jerusalem seemed on the whole to be the most appropriate. In several passages, however, the German translation used by the author differs significantly from the Jerusalem text, and rather than force the original text, I have used different English versions of the Bible; these are indicated where they occur.

For example, on p. 4 the author's German is more literally a translation of the Greek (Mk 9:24) than the Jerusalem Bible. While the latter, in common with other modern versions (e.g. Phillips, NEB), translates with a periphrasis, a number of modern English versions give a more literal translation (e.g. RSV, Knox, Westminster, Moffatt), and of these I have selected the RSV. Again, Jn 8:25 (quoted on p. 58) is variously interpreted by the King James, Challenor, RSV, Westminster, Phillips, Jerusalem, etc. The NEB and Knox give the sense of 'Why should I bother speaking to you at all?' As this reading is pertinent to the particular passage in which the quotation occurs, I have in this case based the translation of the whole essay on the NEB. Again, on p. 82 none of the modern English versions gives the sense of

Jn 3:8 intended by the author. I have therefore had to resort to the Douay.

Other slight divergences of the German from the Jerusalem Bible, where the sense is not affected, have not been mentioned.

Foreword

In his letter to the Christians at Rome, Paul writes that he wishes to strengthen them 'by sharing a spiritual gift, or what is better, to find encouragement among [them] from their common faith' (Rm 1:11–12). At a time of upheaval and unrest, a similar wish moves me to offer the following pages. These days people are keen on 'critical dialogue', which often turns out to be just straight confrontation; spiritual dialogue is less frequent, but still of vital importance to the life of faith.

The reader will find grouped together here lectures, conferences, addresses and shorter publications which have all been revised for the purposes of this collective volume. Different literary 'genres' have deliberately been selected: reflections, meditations (based on various biblical passages), three sermons or homilies, and at the end a personal profession of faith drawn up at the request of a group of priests. All these works necessarily betray my own particular way of looking at things, and I fully acknowledge that limitation.

As I write I have many Christians in mind who have talked over the faith with me, and who have brought Paul's words on exchange and mutual encouragement to life. If other Christians who come to read this book receive similar encouragement, they may thank all those who, by their agreement and criticism, their questions and their insights, have contributed to it.

Würzburg, 20.8.1972   *The Author*

Faith in Times of Temptation

It has been said that there are no unbelievers in whom there is not some trace of belief, and no believers without their share of unbelief. As far as self-declared unbelievers are concerned, the question may be left undecided here. But the believer, if he is honest with himself, might well agree: side by side with belief there is doubt in his heart—disbelief troubles him, intrudes into his inmost thoughts and throws his orderly faith into confusion. Sometimes a single chance word heard from those around him is enough to unsettle him, at others he is overwhelmed with disappointments and his faith begins to waver. Doubt, uncertainty, temptation loom up on the believer's horizon in many different guises.

Similar experiences have been a commonplace since the very earliest times of Christianity. Even the disciples were not spared while Jesus was still with them. What did they really think and believe about him at that time? We cannot say exactly, because all the Gospels were written in the light of their Easter faith. But the evangelists do not conceal the fact that the disciples' faith before the resurrection was undiscerning and shaky, a prey to trial and temptation. They even

1

emphasise this, to show later believers how they could learn to cope in similar situations.

There is a scene certainly based on a historical event which shows the disciples in serious difficulty: they are trying to cure an epileptic boy in Jesus's absence, but meet with no success (Mk 9:14–18 and par.) If we remember that when Jesus sent them out two by two into the surrounding villages he had given them power to drive out devils and cure all forms of illness (cf. Mk 6: 7 and 13), and that, as Luke explains, when they came back almost dancing with joy they could announce that even the devils submitted to them when they used Jesus's name (Lk 10:17), then we can understand something of the shock they must have experienced at their humiliating failure. Even this little story is related unsparingly to the community so that they could learn from it. Mark tells how, after Jesus had cured the boy himself, the disciples asked him privately, 'Why were we unable to cast the devil out?', and Jesus replied: 'This is the kind that can only be driven out by prayer' (Mk 9:28–29). This saying of Jesus has often been misunderstood, as if faith alone were not enough, but intensive prayer needed as well. Early copyists added 'and fasting'. They obviously thought that prayer gained even greater effectiveness if it went hand in hand with fasting. Jesus himself, however, specifically stated to the boy's father: 'Everything is possible for anyone who has faith' (Mk 9:23). This is to say that to a belief that is strong enough nothing is out of reach. Such a state is arrived at through prayer—so Mark rightly explains it for his readers.

We can come even closer to the evangelist's thought here if we turn to another passage of his Gospel in

2

which he talks even more insistently about the need for faith and prayer together. After the cursing of the fig-tree, he juxtaposes the two sayings about faith moving mountains and prayer that is certain to be granted (Mk 11:23–24) in such a way that they illuminate and complement each other. There is a type of unshakeable, charismatic faith which can achieve through God what humanly speaking must be written off as impossible; faith like this, however, is a gift from God which one can only implore in prayer. And there is a type of prayer which is sure to be rewarded, and this presumes a faith that is quite free of all doubting. There is a dialectic here: belief and prayer condition each other mutually in a fruitful tension. Faith grows in prayer, and prayer requires a living faith. Luke reports the saying on charismatic faith in a slightly different tradition: 'Were your faith the size of a mustard seed you could say to this mulberry tree, "Be uprooted and planted in the sea", and it would obey you' (17:6). But Luke too recognises the extraordinary nature of this kind of faith, and makes the disciples preface Christ's words with the request: 'Increase our faith' (17:5), One can only pray for faith such as this.

Paul also knows of this faith that can move mountains (1 Co 13:2), an indication that Jesus's words reported in Mk 11:23 had sunk deep into the Church's consciousness and had been faithfully passed on. For Paul, too, this faith is a charism, a special gift from the Spirit. If the early Church received great charismatic blessings, such as extraordinary powers of healing (cf. 1 Co 12:9 and 28), our passage in Mark testifies that this was not always so. They would become more conscious of their own weakness and better appreciate that

3

prayer and patience are necessary too.

This, then, was the conviction of the early Christians on the basis of Jesus's own teaching about faith and prayer. We must all confess that if we face up to it honestly, the saying raises considerable difficulties for our own faith even when we make no attempt to apply it to concrete situations in our lives. It would be presumptuous to use it to extort, as it were, a charismatic faith or a doubt-free prayer. Neither can be extorted or manipulated; they are bestowed in exceptional cases only. They were certainly given to many of the saints: *Deus mirabilis est in sanctis suis* (God is wonderful in his saints, Ps 67:36, Vulg. and Douay).

The coexistence of belief with unbelief is expressed in the exclamation recorded of the unfortunate boy's father: 'I believe, help my unbelief' (Mk 9:24, RSV). This is one of those 'existential' saying in the Gospels which has a remarkable appeal in our own situation. The man has a burning desire to believe and yet is only too conscious of the frailty of his belief. We can say more: he knows that it is easier for unbelief to find a lodging in his heart, and that belief, if it is to come at all, must be a gift from the all-merciful God, beyond his own strength to acquire. So his answer is an urgent prayer.

There is no unbroken and untroubled faith without the grace of God. Only he can turn our faith into unshakeable and resolute certainty. In this world as we see it, with its obscure and ambiguous surface, in the darkness of suffering and evil, in the midst of other men's unbelief, not even the believer can remain untouched by uncertainty and doubt.

There are other places in Mark's Gospel which give

4

us glimpses of the difficulties in faith encountered by
the community for which he is writing. We hear quite a
lot about the disciples' stubbornness and lack of true
understanding. On one occasion Jesus warns them:
'Are your minds closed? Have you eyes that do not
see, ears that do not hear?' (8:17–18). The community
were especially slow to grasp that Jesus's death by
crucifixion was decreed by God, and that they themselves would be called on to follow in the same way of
the Cross (cf. 8:32–38). They would have to suffer per-
secutions for the sake of Jesus's name (cf. 13:9–13),
false prophets would arise to spark off a sham epidemic
of apocalyptic expectation (cf. 13:21–22). But Mark
urges them to persevere and be watchful; the end is not
yet. We should like to see for ourselves something of
the might of Christ and the splendour of his resurrection; but instead God invites us on the way of the
Cross, in the darkness of pain.

One's own temptations in faith also lead to a greater
appreciation of the lack of faith in others. A faith
which is sure of itself runs the risk of becoming intolerant and harsh. This is why Mark's Gospel gives an example on this point which arises from a profound reflection on the problems of faith. John the son of
Zebedee once said to Jesus: 'Master, we saw a man
who is not one of us casting out devils in your name;
and because he was not one of us we tried to stop him.'
Jesus replied: 'You must not stop him: no one who
works a miracle in my name is likely to speak evil of
me. Anyone who is not against us is for us' (9:38–40).
We find in these words of Jesus a generosity and a
tolerance not often met with today. But conduct like
this obviously existed in the early Church, which had

5

already in its life and missionary endeavour come up against 'outsiders' and aliens. Today's troubled times compel us, with the disciples and early Church, to meditate a great deal on the faith. We are all tempted; we can only pray: 'Lord, I believe, help my unbelief.'

Plurality and Unity in the Faith

Plurality of opinion and behaviour in the Church today is considered by some Christians to be nothing less than an assault on the Church's very unity. Such massive criticism as we are experiencing today of bishops' decisions, Church leaders' methods and teachings was unthinkable a decade ago. At least, in questions of faith there was very little publicity given to a discussion. The various theological opinions were left to theologians to fight over, and such debate as there was, was confined to academic circles. Now not only do strange, new-fangled ideas ('modern theology') cause unrest, but the monolithic structure of Christian doctrine threatens to crumble into fragments. Is there not great cause for bewilderment in the Church when its belief seems to be disintegrating into a host of disparate interpretations and explanations? And this sorrow at losing the strength that comes from tight unity is by no means the acutest; there is a challenge to the faith itself : should such things be in the one, Catholic and apostolic Church? In such a situation as this, it is useful to take a look back at the early Church and the evidence of the New Testament.

The differences and antagonisms in the primitive Christian community were probably in fact much greater than we usually imagine. Yet Christians clung tenaciously to one conviction: there is 'one Lord, one faith, one baptism, and one God who is Father of all' (Ep 4:5-6). They held fast to the eucharistic gathering, associated fraternally with each other, supported poorer communities by having collections, and gave hospitality to wandering missionaries or other Christians who came their way. There was in other words a plurality which did not disturb the overall unity.

There is more behind the dispute between the 'Hebrews' and the 'Hellenists' in the early community in Jerusalem (Ac 6:1-6) than simple disagreement over the care of widows. The 'Seven' were not deacons who just saw to the distribution of food and left the proclamation of the Gospel to the 'Twelve', but more than probably the leaders of the Jewish-Hellenist community. For example, we know that Stephen was an eloquent preacher (Ac 6:9-10); Philip was active as a wandering missionary and could boast of significant successes in Samaria (8:1-8) and the coastal cities of Palestine up to Caesarea (8:26-40). But a close analysis of Stephen's speech in Ac 7 makes it clear that these two leaders of the Hellenic Christians took a theological view of the Jewish Law (cf. 6:14) and the Jerusalem temple which differed considerably from that of the other apostles. The 'Hellenists' were persecuted and fled; the 'Apostles' were allowed to stay in Jerusalem (8:1).

The position with regard to Judaism was a crucial question for the early Church, involving as it did basic theological principles. The bone of contention at the 'Apostles' Council' (Ac 15) is well-known: were Gentiles who came over to Christianity to be circumcised or

8

not? The assembly decided against the strict Judaisers who were keen to retain the ancient Jewish practice. But even after this there were lots of problems when it came to associating with the Jewish Christians who openly continued to practise the Jewish Law even when fraternising with their Christian brothers who were Gentile converts. In modern language we could perhaps refer to a 'post-conciliar' situation. It came to a head in the 'Antioch incident' or the confrontation between Paul and Peter (Ga 2:11–14). In the flourishing community at Antioch, which was the metropolis of the Gentile missionary effort, sharing a table with the Gentile Christians was at first unobjectionable in the mind of the Jewish Christians. Only when strictly law-abiding Jewish Christians came from Jerusalem did the Antiochene Jewish Christians segregate themselves from their brothers in the faith. Peter's behaviour contributed to the friction, and Paul called him to account 'in front of everyone'. This dispute is not to be thought of as a controversy over small practicalities: for Paul at any rate the very truth of his Gospel to the Gentiles, an inalienable part of which was freedom from the Law and circumcision, was at stake (cf. 2: 15–21).

There are other examples of theological tension in the early Church, for instance over the expectation of an imminent parousia and the 'apocalyptic' thinking that characterised many primitive Christian circles. But in John the parousia recedes altogether: for him salvation is already here in the present Christ. We could speak of a 'demythologisation'. John therefore at all events had quite a different emphasis, and developed a Christian theology which to the other circles was suspect and even a cause of scandal. Was salvation present or to come? Was salvation mediated through the sacraments or through a personal offering of faith? Should Christians look back to the historical Jesus or concentrate on the ever-present exalted Christ? These are questions which are still, or again, with us today. Even the different conceptions of 'belief and works' in Paul and James are not to be overlooked. True, the two theologians are not in contradiction, but their viewpoints are rather different, and their ways of expression are so unlike that they seem to be talking completely at variance. Many more cases could be quoted besides.

The early Church in fact knew different 'theologies', but the factions did not for that accuse each other of heresy. It was not just orthopraxis (agreement in matters of practical Christian conduct) which held the community together; but Christians looked more closely at orthodoxy (right belief) only when dangerous false teaching—coupled with false unChristian behaviour—threatened the community's stability. In those times they were satisfied with brief formulas of faith, which expressed the essential core: confession of Jesus Christ as the Saviour. Those who confessed him submitted to him as their Lord whose instructions they were anxious to follow. Belief and life, for these first Christians, went inextricably hand in hand. Paul once formulated it as follows, with reference particularly to baptism: 'If your lips confess that Jesus is Lord and if you believe in your heart that God raised him from the dead, then you will be saved' (Rm 10:9).

This justifies the modern desire to appreciate the truths of faith at their proper value, to put them in the right perspective in their own world of origin, and to reach a short formula of belief for one's own time. It is a question of preserving and expressing what is central, essential and indispensable in the Christian faith. Once that has happened, other more peripheral expressions of faith, possibly quite fruitful at one time but now less significant, can be soft-pedalled. To fit into the mental horizon of modern man, there is much that must be reformulated. Similar changes take place in the practice of the faith, in expressions of personal piety, and in collective worship. Often, quite unexpectedly and unpredictably, feelings change and new forms of expression emerge. A new generation looks for new ways of expressing its approach to life. This is not to be deplored; on the contrary, it is a sign of the faith's vitality, of its indestructible strength even in vastly altered circumstances. The only thing is that Jesus Christ, the goal and centre of the Christian faith, must at all times be in total evidence.

Therefore we must have greater understanding not only for the difficulties many fellow-Christians experience in their faith, but also for the quite different pattern of their thinking. Should we measure whether and how much they come up to the old articulations of the faith? Should we pass judgement if they satisfy only a part of the requirements? It is not always very clear when and on what grounds early Christian communities excluded individual members or whole groups from their fellowship. John's first letter lays down one or two 'principles' (which are in fact only suggestions) which concern the most vital Christian affirmation (cf. 2:22–23; 4:2–3; 5:5–6). For the most part, it seems, the early communities were reluctant to take disciplinary measures. A profound insight and strength lies behind John's words on stray members: 'If [those rivals of Christ] had belonged, they would have stayed with us; but they left us, to prove that not one of them ever belonged to us' (1 Jn 2:19). Do we not trust the Holy Spirit sufficiently to carry out the necessary discernment of spirits and to remove 'those that do not belong'? Do we really have to be so worried about 'the Trojan horse in the Church' that we set up funeral pyres before we are quite certain in our own minds who in fact are the false brothers who 'have furtively crept in' (cf. Ga 2:4)? Politics in history furnish more than enough examples of how hazardous ideological purges can be. We must beware of 'conformity with this world' (cf. Rm 12:2) in this regard too if we do not wish to betray the freedom won for us by Christ. 'Our war is not fought with weapons of flesh, yet [our weapons] are strong enough, in God's cause, to demolish fortresses' (2 Co 10:4).

If we hanker after an orthodox uniformity in the Christian faith (which in any case was often more present on people's lips than in their heads and hearts), that, too, in its own way, is smallness and frailty of faith. True unity in faith is not at man's beck and call, and while we are in history can only be approached at a distance. At the present moment we must possibly satisfy ourselves with remembering, in Paul's words, that 'nobody can lay any other [foundation] than the one which has already been laid, that is Jesus Christ' (1 Co 3:11). The Spirit of Jesus will tell one spirit from another, unmasking those who do not belong, and uniting those who do, even though at the moment, in appearance, they are divided from us.

Belief in Jesus Christ

The name and title of the Man from Nazareth pose in a concise form the most basic problem of the Christian confession of faith. 'Jesus' refers to this particular historical man who lived in a particular place, Palestine, at a particular time in man's history. 'Christ', which is the Greek translation of the Hebrew *maschiach* (= one who has been anointed), is a designation for the Saviour so long looked forward to by the Jews, although many widely differing ideas were current as to the type of person he would be. When the early Jewish Christians announced that '*Jesus* is the Messiah', it was, in the Judaic mentality of that period, a statement of belief of the first importance. The most common Jewish notion of the Messiah was that of the 'Son of David', a Ruler from royal stock who would re-establish Israel's earthly kingdom and make it an ideal kingdom of peace and justice. This, however, was not at all the Messiah whom Christians acknowledged and professed in Jesus of Nazareth. This 'prophet from Galilee' was a simple man of the people, poor like most of the peasantry, living with the neediest, and identifying himself with the oppressed and the under-privileged. On top of this, the ruling circles of his own people hounded

13

him and brought him finally to the Cross. He died the fearful death of crucifixion, a man accursed. It was the Christian conviction that this crucified man was God's Anointed, the long-awaited Saviour from whom all deliverance was to come.

To proclaim to the Jewish people belief in a Messiah of this sort was far from being an easy matter. We know how Jesus's followers, themselves Jews by birth and mentality, proved their claim: it was because God raised the crucified Jesus from the dead and 'made him both Lord and Christ' (Ac 2:36). They applied to him the words of Ps 110: 'Yahweh's oracle to you, my Lord, "Sit at my right hand and I will make your enemies a footstool for you"' (v. 1).

This was how the early Jewish Christians tried to explain to 'the whole house of Israel' how this man from Galilee, outwardly so little like a Messiah, was in fact, by God's hidden plan, the expected Saviour, the 'Ruler' in a much deeper sense than the Jews had ever dreamed of. The carpenter's son who had been rejected by men was accepted and acknowledged by God and became for all who believe in him 'the prince of life' (Ac 3:15).

The first Christians then amplified their confession of Jesus as Messiah by adding new titles, one of the most important of which was 'Son of God'. In John's Gospel, Nathaniel exclaims: 'Rabbi, you are the Son of God, you are the King of Israel' (1:49), and Martha confesses: 'I believe that you are the Christ, the Son of God, the one who was to come into this world' (11:27). This is the creed of the Johannine community (cf. 20:31); the whole of John's Gospel is an attempt to demonstrate its reasonableness and its cogency, and to

14

convince his readers of it by the words and events of Jesus that he records.

Today the problem of this confession of Jesus as the Christ presents itself to us in a somewhat different form. How can this historical man Jesus of Nazareth be of absolute significance for all men? Everything that belongs to our human history we consider to be conditioned and limited, repeatable and transitory. Is it not an inescapable part of what it means to be human that each individual is only a tiny fraction of mankind and plays a restricted, time-conditioned role, however great he may once have been and however long the period of his influence? How can one particular man be credited with a unique significance for all men, and in a sense so pregnant that the eternal salvation of every man depends on him? The first Christians asserted nothing less than this when they proclaimed that 'of all the names in the world given to men, this is the only one by which we can be saved' (Ac 4 : 12). This is precisely the paradox of our faith, the stumbling-block of absurdity and inconsequence, which receives its most concise and striking formulation in John's Prologue: 'The Word was made flesh' (1 : 14), which is to say that the eternal, the invisible, the absolute, the infinite, the unbelievable became, in this man Jesus of Nazareth, an earthly, historical, palpable reality. 'Something which has existed since the beginning, that we have heard, and we have seen with our own eyes; that we have watched and touched with our hands—this is our subject' (1 Jn 1 : 1). Since then, for all these centuries, Christian theology has been wrestling with this mystery of the incarnation. To modern man it sounds like a myth to say that God sent his only Son into the world, that this Son became man, suffered and died, but then, raised up by God and exalted to power, achieved once again the glory that was his from the beginning (cf. Jn 17:5 and 24).

What is the meaning of all these statements about Jesus being the Christ and the Son of God? Can we make this central Christian mystery more accessible to modern man, or must it for ever far exceed the capacities of human understanding? First of all, we have to be sure that however the Christological statements are articulated, they are not made for their own sake. They are not abstract speculations about Christ or ponderings on the mysteries as such. They are made to move and inspire us, as the Johannine Prologue makes clear: 'From his fulness we have, all of us, received ... grace in return for grace' (1:16). But that said, they are still hard to understand; can we explain them today in easier language? What does belief in Jesus Christ the Son of God mean for us and our humanity?

There is no doubt that just like the first Christians who followed Jesus while he was still alive we have to begin with the man Jesus of Nazareth. It is he who in his uniqueness and special significance gives the Christian faith its unmistakable stamp. Gods, divine creatures and divinised men are common in many religions; but this man from Nazareth, who was crucified under Pontius Pilate, is totally different from what previous ages have understood by divinised human beings (even when Hellenistic Christians sometimes attempted to attribute such traits to Christ). Jesus was, as we might say, so human, so obviously and fully a man from among men, that all attempts to understand him as a mere cultic divinity or a myth are bound to fail. When

Christianity began penetrating circles in which Hellenistic culture was predominant, there was, it is true, a real danger of turning Jesus into a divinised hero or a cultic figure; but that corner-stone of Christian belief— that the earthly, historical Jesus of Nazareth is the Christ—was not to be so easily dislodged. And even when in later centuries sporadic attempts were made by some Christians to talk exclusively or even predominantly in terms of a divine redeemer, the assurance of Jesus's humanity, of his solid appearance in human history, of his words and deeds, his suffering and his dying, could never founder.

Today the figure of this historical Jesus of Nazareth is once again very close to our hearts. Even young people who no longer care very much for institutional Christianity are rediscovering him. Many see in him a man who exploded all the social conventions of his time, who took on himself the cause of the oppressed and the outcast, who dared to challenge the mighty and the powerful in the land, and so he becomes a social outsider and a revolutionary. Others feel that this way of conceiving Jesus does not really grasp the actual historical reality. He was not a revolutionary who called his followers to arms; he unequivocally opposed violence, and he forbade revenge. His sole weapons were free, fearless and incorruptible speech, and a completely impartial attitude to the highly-placed and the humble, the rich and the poor. His message was the coming of God's kingdom of love and peace, his charge corresponding love between man and man of whatever class, particularly towards the unfortunate and the ill-treated. Everything the Gospels relate about him speaks of a total disinterest in men's judgement of him,

17

a true freedom which arises from the certainty of his divine mission and gives him a conviction of his own 'authority' (cf. Mk 1:22; 11:28). Even critical science, which for a long time ventured to say little or nothing about the historical Jesus because of the alleged insufficiency of our sources, and the distortion due to the disciples' Easter experience and the evangelists' obtruding personal views, is beginning to see that it must alter its position if it is in any way credibly to explain the rise of Christianity, the peculiar nature of primitive Christian preaching (the 'kerygma'), and the conduct of the first communities.

Yet it is not at all easy, it must be said, to give a clear and adequate picture of the historical Jesus. Nineteenth-century investigations into Jesus's life are a sufficient warning. They admirably illustrate the danger of creating Jesus in one's own image and likeness, of fitting him into a ready-made pattern. The nineteenth century produced all sorts of different tableaux of the Man from Nazareth: romantic, pietist, socialist, political, psychological and others, which A. Schweitzer's *The Quest of the Historical Jesus* (1906) finally showed up in all their inadequacy. It is to be feared that many modern books on Jesus now in vogue run the same risk. Is it perhaps our sources, the Gospels, which are at fault for not having given us a biography and a portrait? But if we stop concentrating on externals and look instead for Jesus's deeper intentions and the reason for his special individual style of life, then we begin to understand that already to his contemporaries, even his closest disciples, he was to a large extent an unknown quantity.

The evangelists were unable to conjure up for their

readers an adequate picture of the historical Jesus, and they surely did not wish to, less because of a paucity of details in the traditions than because of the impossibility of faithfully portraying the historical figure. They were themselves convinced that the true Jesus was disclosed to them only in the light of faith. But also, behind their accounts (indeed some pericopes explicitly say so) we sense their contemporaries' inability to come to any conclusion as to the person and manner of Jesus. He cannot be forced into any preconceived category, whether it be popular preacher, healer and wonder-worker, prophet, liberator, revolutionary or even Messiah. Even comparisons with the great figures of Judaism, and the expectations current at the time, open up no satisfactory horizons, give no satisfactory answers. One thing only comes unmistakably through all the accounts: the hidden strength which nourished the whole of Jesus's speaking and doing was his relationship to God; he was, in the very deepest sense, a 'man of God'. The precise way in which he was this began to dawn on his disciples from the moment they became aware that the Crucified was risen. And then it was just as hard to find suitable classification for this man killed by men and raised by God.

Nevertheless, on the basis of all the aspects of Jesus we glimpse through the Gospel narratives, it is possible to say something that brings him closer to us today. His message of love, substantiated by his own attitudes and actions, indeed his whole life, and his demand for a similar love in others, are beyond dispute. Solely on this one score, with all its implications for interhuman and social relationships and for man's self-understanding, Jesus of Nazareth achieves an imperishable significance

19

for mankind, in our own time as well. And if modern man calls this his message from God, he can grasp something of who God is too. Jesus is giving credibility not only to a doctrine of God, but to the authentic presence of God himself in this man Jesus. In him God has approached, communicated himself, and given himself to man.

Certainly only those who already believe in Jesus Christ will understand that in Jesus God has taken all humanity irrevocably and definitively up into his love. Only he who accepts the primitive Christian confession that Jesus is the Christ whom God, after the death on the Cross, acknowledged and affirmed as his beloved Son sent into the world for man's salvation, can fully see and appreciate Jesus Christ's unique significance for all men. This is because his true and final meaning lies not in a humanitarian doctrine, however important, or in his example and the encouragement given by his own way of life, but actually in his person. This, for the believer, is not a historical enigma from the past, but a living presence for us now, opening up and guaranteeing our future as one of impending salvation.

David's Scion and the Child in the Manger

Lk 1: 31–33

> *Listen! You are to conceive and bear a son, and you must name him Jesus.*
>
> *He will be great and will be called Son of the Most High.*
>
> *The Lord God will give him the throne of his ancestor David;*
>
>> *he will rule over the House of Jacob for ever and his reign will have no end.*

In these words, recorded by Luke in the angel's address to Mary when he announced that although a virgin she would give birth to a child, we are struck by the mention of the Saviour's royal ancestry. The description of the birth itself is in remarkable contrast (Lk 2): the boy promised by the angel is born in extreme poverty, a child in a manger, and yet God's message to the shepherds on the hillside speaks of this child as the long-awaited Messiah: 'Today in the town of David a saviour has been born to you; he is Christ the Lord' (2:11). Son of a king, ruler in his own right, and child in a feeding-trough: what can it all mean? Luke is evidently conscious of the paradox, but as the repeated reference to David and his city of Bethlehem clearly shows, he is sure of his ground.

There is a probable explanation: for his annunciation scene, the evangelist simply takes over a previous account, probably the product of an early Jewish Christian community. The purpose of this document or tradition is to depict Jesus as the promised scion of David's house with all the royal and princely attributes which according to the Old Testament prophets were to be his. Luke then accepts this idea and incorporates it into his christology without seeing any contradiction between that and Jesus's birth in poverty and his death on the Cross. For Luke the angel's words are fulfilled at the resurrection and exaltation at God's right hand. This underlying theology comes through clearly in Ac 2:34-36, where Peter says, with a reference to Ps 110: 1: 'For this reason the whole House of Israel can be certain that God has made this Jesus whom you crucified both Lord and Christ.' Jesus is seen as the kingly ruler, to whom God has subjugated all his enemies, not in his earthly living and dying, but in his resurrection. His dominion, which will have no end, is not a wielding of earthly authority and power, but a spiritual rule of blessing which will come to all who believe in the resurrection of their crucified Lord.

This understanding was of decisive importance for the development of early Christianity. The Jewish expectancy of a glorious, earthly Messiah, which contrasted so sharply with the actual historical facts of the

22

earthly Jesus and the primitive Christian faith in his messianism, was suddenly brought into harmony with them. But we may wonder what those early Jewish Christians who first formulated the primitive account really thought of Christ's kingship. The texts alluded to in the announcing angel's words (Is 7:14; 2 S 7:13 and 16) all refer to an earthly kingdom for the Messiah. He will 'sit on the throne of his father David', and he will reign for ever 'over the House of Jacob' (= Israel). Did they think that Jesus would return and establish his earthly kingdom of peace and justice then? Or were they expecting at least a partial realisation of Christ's kingdom of peace, with an influence already there and then to which they themselves would contribute? They evidently regarded themselves as the true Israel in whom, through Jesus, the old promises were fulfilled: Jesus would reign for ever over the House of Jacob. But how was this reign to materialise?

In Jewish thought, God's salvation was not, or at least not only and not primarily, a transcendent affair, because it involved the transformation of earthly relationships, indeed of all human existence, from within. It would also be a misunderstanding of the Christian message to deny the kingdom of Christ and God any relation with this world, as if it were merely a promise for the future, a dream and a comfort after all the misery of human history. Christ is the Lord who is present here and now, permeating the existing world with 'righteousness and peace and joy brought by the Holy Spirit' (Rm 14:17)—in the life and conduct of his disciples, in the work of his people throughout the world. Other nations too can be included in this basically Jewish picture. The old man Simeon praises God in the temple: 'My eyes have seen the salvation which you have prepared for all the nations to see, a light to enlighten the pagans and the glory of your people Israel' (Lk 2: 30–32).

But to talk about Christ's reign at all can be misleading: it could give rise to a triumphalistic understanding of history and the Church. So we find that Luke's nativity story guards against this danger by drawing attention to the opposite: the Son of the Most High is born, a helpless infant, to poverty. This Saviour is near to men in their need and misery; through him they can come to know God's thoughts; through him God's call to love and compassion rings out unmistakably. This man Jesus has taken on himself our own weaknesses, he has experienced human wretchedness for himself, and he has suffered grief and pain in his own body.

To bestow this Saviour on us, God chose the obedient and humble Virgin Mary. For Luke this is an integral part of the annunciation story: the maiden will conceive through the power of the Holy Spirit and so fulfil the promises of Isaiah about Immanuel, God-with-us. She must call her child 'Jesus', which means 'Yahweh saves'. In him God comes to us, he is with us, speaks to us about his love and salvation, and from that there is no turning back. So God's 'kingdom' is quite different from an exercise of secular authority over men: it is not force and power, but liberating love and the capacity to love, an invitation to freedom in love. Jesus has established his kingdom for ever among men who, like Mary, affirm it with their Fiat.

God's Plans for Revolution

Lk 1: 51–55

> *He has shown the power of his arm,*
> *he has routed the proud of heart.*
> *He has pulled down princes from their thrones and*
> *exalted the lowly.*
> *The hungry he has filled with good things, the rich sent*
> *empty away.*
> *He has come to the help of Israel his servant,*
> *mindful of his mercy—*
> *according to the promise he made to our ancestors—*
> *of his mercy to Abraham and to his descendants for ever.*

These sentences from the Magnificat, Mary's song of praise, can be extremely helpful when we come to meditate on the deeper meaning of Christmas. It has been suggested that the Magnificat was originally Mary's hymn of thanksgiving *after* the birth of her Son, and that the evangelist, on purely literary grounds, transferred it to *before* the birth, when Mary visited her cousin Elizabeth. This cannot be proved, as there is no sure evidence of the origin of the song. In any case we need not dwell on that question here as it does not affect the meaning of the words we are considering. When the angel tells Mary of her mysterious motherhood, she is filled with wonder at God's ways, and acknowledges the mysteriousness of his actions beyond all human criteria and expectations. God is not limited to man's notions of power and greatness, but chooses for his purposes what in the world's eyes is weak and of little account (cf. 1 Co 1:27–28). Mary's case is no different. She is only too well aware of her own humble life, and yet still she is called to bring Israel its awaited Saviour. From this awareness, expressed in the first strophe of the song (1:46–50), grows her prophetic certainty that God will bring messianic salvation too in just the same way. This is the meaning of the second strophe of the Magnificat.

God will revolutionise the world's existing conditions of deception and injustice. The use of the past tense in the Magnificat, which is in a way rather surprising, does not refer back to Israel's history, or even express a universal experience of how God acts, but is describing the future in terms of the past 'because the future fulfilment of God's promises is foreshadowed and guaranteed by the past' (H. Schürmann). At the same time Mary remembers God's wise and secret action in the past. Her words remind us of the song sung by Hannah, Samuel's mother, who had a similar experience to Mary's. Defying all human expectations, God gave her a son in her barrenness. 'The sated hire themselves out for bread but the famished cease from labour; the barren woman bears sevenfold, but the mother of many is desolate.... Yahweh makes poor and rich, he humbles

26

and also exalts. He raises the poor from the dust, he lifts the needy from the dunghill to give them a place with princes' (1 S 2 : 5–8). This son of hers, Samuel, whom she and her husband gave to the temple service at Shiloh, was a seer and a prophetic leader in Israel. Mary was to be the mother of the longed-for Messiah from whom was to come God's final salvation.

Mary is quite certain that God will work his rescue of man in this 'paradoxical' way, so baffling to human calculation. 'He has pulled down princes from their thrones and exalted the lowly. The hungry he has filled with good things, the rich sent empty away.' From this it almost seems as if a political and social revolution is announced; but we must say once again that there can be no reference here to revolution by force. The Messiah is not a war hero and a judge of nations, his work cannot really be described; only one thing is certain: through him God will unexpectedly change many things, and will take to himself the poor and the distressed.

God's ways are ways of mercy. At the end of the first strophe, Mary remarked: 'His mercy reaches from age to age for those who fear him.' Now she takes up this thought again: '[God] has come to the help of Israel his servant, mindful of his mercy—according to the promise he made to our ancestors—of his mercy . . . for ever.' The Messiah-child is the pledge of God's compassion to man. However poor and frail he comes into the world, he is the proof of God's power to save and of his never-ending pity. The particular way in which God will accomplish his purposes is kept secret from Mary. This, too, is characteristic of God, that the fulfilment is different from the expectation.

Is Mary's confident, joyful celebration mere pious ideology, a utopian belief in a world where brute force and injustice, the insolence of the rich and the misery of the poor still proliferate? This may seem so to those who do not believe in the power of divine love brought into the world by Jesus. But those who look on Jesus's living and dying and understand that his love is not weakness and his death not defeat will see something of that revolutionary, subverting action of God which Mary celebrated prophetically in her song of thanksgiving.

The Precursor

Mk 1: 1–3

*The beginning of the Good News about Jesus
Christ, the Son of God.*
It is written in the book of the prophet Isaiah:
*Look, I am going to send my messenger before
you;*
he will prepare your way.
A voice cries in the wilderness:
Prepare a way for the Lord,
make his paths straight.

In the mind of the earliest evangelist, John the Baptist
is not the last flicker of God's Old Covenant; he most
definitely belongs to the new one. He is the beginning
of God's Good News of salvation, of the Gospel, because his ministry leads directly to that of Jesus of
Nazareth who is to fulfil God's plans. His fascinating
figure, which brought a popular Jewish movement into
being, strongly exercised the minds of the Christian
community as well. In manner he was quite different

from Jesus: austere and stern, announcing God's imminent judgement and fearlessly forcing his contemporaries' attention on their sins, especially those of the influential and powerful. Jesus seemed to be different: a messenger of joy who turned to the poor and oppressed and promised *them* God's love, even going so far as to sit at table with despised tax collectors (cf. Mt 11:18–19). There were circles in primitive Christianity who considered that the man of self-denial and penance still belonged to the Old Testament, even if he was one of the greatest of the prophets. But for Mark he is the voice who, although in a contrasting key, preludes Jesus's Gospel, a messenger from God who prepares the work of his Messiah, and ultimately, in his brutal death, a sign of the destiny to be suffered by the Son of Man himself (cf. Mk 9:12–13).

Primitive Christian reflection in the New Testament is witnessed by these quotations even before the explicit description of the baptist and his ministry. His prophetic figure is cast in a definite light; he is the expected second Elijah who according to Malachi is to appear as God's messenger to prepare the way (Ml 3:1). Christians apply to their Messiah statements originally made about God: God comes when Jesus Christ comes ('before *you*'). In the following quotation, too, from the Book of Isaiah, the word 'Lord', originally addressed to Yahweh, is applied to Jesus: *he* is the one who is coming, the one more powerful than John, the one who will baptise with the Holy Spirit (cf. 1:7–8). The combined scriptural quotations, attributed jointly to Isaiah, show how free the early Church was in its use of Scripture. They read Scripture backwards, one might say, from the event that was Jesus, and understood the event as the fulfilment of Scripture, the product of divine planning of a piece with the Old Testament, and this gave it meaning. Not until then did the unusual phenomenon of John, the priest's son, become intelligible. He is Elijah, the last messenger of the Lord's appearance, a voice crying in the wilderness. What in the original prophecy was only an image, an impersonal voice announcing to the people the Lord's mighty and salvific coming, now takes on visible reality and palpable form. What was originally described was only God's royal path, a wide and even road through the desert ('Prepare a way in the wilderness'); here it is the messenger who appears in the desert ('A voice cries in the wilderness'). His appearance is a symbol and a challenge. The mention of 'wilderness' has many associations. The strict Qumran sect used the same passage from Isaiah to justify and express their seclusion in the desert 'separated from the dwellings of unrighteous men' in strictest obedience to the Law and in the greatest purity as a preparation for God's coming (Qumran Rule 8:13 f.). The desert is also a place where God is near and where he reveals himself, e.g. to the prophet Elijah (1 K 19:4-9), and a place of promise, since Israel's period of wandering in the desert was seen as a time of grace which prefigured the future era of salvation. In Mark's Gospel, at all events, the desert is a place of redemption, and John, the man of the desert, is, despite all his ascetic ways, a harbinger of salvation.

The Baptist did not withdraw himself from men, but spoke to them from near a ford over the Jordan. But to hear him one had to turn aside a little from busy haunts to the quiet spot where he was baptising.

Crowds went to him because they felt the strength that emanated from this man of God: not a reed swaying in the breeze or a man wearing fine clothes (cf. Mt 11: 7–8), but one who issued forth from solitude and stillness, and untouched by the world's traffic and the opinion of men, pointed out the road to salvation. His was a persuasive call, because he himself heeded the call of God. He was a messenger from the desert who ventured into the busy and heedless bustle of men; a finger of God extended to point out the One to come who was greater than he.

Someone More Powerful than John

Mk 1: 7–8

> *In the course of his preaching [John] said,*
> *'Someone is following me, someone who is more power-*
> *ful than I am, and I am not fit to kneel down and undo*
> *the strap of his sandals.*
> *I have baptised you with water,*
> *but he will baptise you with the Holy Spirit.'*

We are no longer in a position historically to discover
all the facts about the relationship between the two extraordinary figures with which Judaism was confronted
at the beginning of the Christian era, John the Baptist
and Jesus of Nazareth. It is clear that the Christian
community saw John's insistence on penance as a preparation for the way of the Messiah, and realised that
it was in Jesus that his prophecies were fulfilled. There
are enough indications, however, that they made a
material distinction between John's preaching and
Jesus's, and we know, for example, that after his death
groups of John's disciples came together and did not

join the Christians (cf. the group of John's disciples at
Ephesus, Ac 19:1–7). There were still circles of the
Baptist's followers as late as the second century, nourished on a belief that John, not Jesus, was the Messiah.
We can be quite sure that this was very far from John's
own mind. None the less his preaching painted a picture of the Messiah which was not easy to square with
the actual reality of Jesus.

In John's mind, God's Anointed was a figure of
power, sweeping the land clean of evil-doers and bringing God's judgement on the wicked. 'His winnowing-
fan is in his hand; he will clear his threshing-floor and
gather his wheat into the barn; but the chaff he will
burn in a fire that will never go out' (Mt 3:12). The
deputation John sent to Jesus from prison (Mt 11:2–5,
and Lk 7:18–22), however we judge its historicity, can
only be understood as showing how puzzled John was
over Jesus's ministry, his healing and his Good News for
the poor and the oppressed: 'Are you the one who is to
come, or have we got to wait for someone else?' There
is no condemnation and no punishment for Jesus, only
the joyful announcement of God's love and mercy for
those who wanted them.

The old tradition on John's preaching preserved for
us in Matthew and Luke throws considerable light on
the passage from Mark given at the head of this
chapter. It relates that the Baptist announced the one
more powerful than himself as one who would baptise
'with the Holy Spirit *and fire*' (Mt 3:11). The exact
background to this 'baptism of fire' is disputed, but it is
almost certainly an image of judgement. In the passage
from Matthew previously quoted, the unquenchable
fire which is to consume the chaff is also an image of

judgement (cf. Is 66:24). Not until later Christian commentary was the baptism prophesied by John limited to 'baptism with the Holy Spirit'. This obviously refers to the outpouring of the Spirit which the Old Testament prophets frequently mention as characteristic of the Last Age. The promise of Jl 3:1–5 is seen by the author of Acts to be fulfilled at Pentecost (Ac 2:17–21). The gift of the Spirit was also connected with baptism 'in the name of Jesus Christ' (Ac 2:38). Thus for the first Christians Jesus was the one who baptised with the Holy Spirit. This primitive Christian understanding provides the exact background to Mark's text.

John's prophetic preaching, which could picture God's power only in violent intervention, condemnation of the wicked and overthrow of unjust earthly institutions, betrayed therein its human limitations, although this does not prevent Jesus from calling the Baptist the greatest 'of all the children born of women' (Mt 11:11). But God's power is beyond man's understanding. He is the Wholly Other whose thoughts are not man's thoughts. His Chosen One is the humble Servant, who 'will not brawl or shout, [whose] voice [is not heard] in the streets', a Saviour who 'will not break the crushed reed, nor put out the smouldering wick', but who none the less 'has led the truth to victory' (Is 42:1–4 quoted as in Mt 12:19–21). This recalls the profound revelation made to the prophet Elijah on Mount Horeb: 'Yahweh himself went by. There came a mighty wind, so strong it tore the mountains and shattered the rocks before Yahweh. But Yahweh was not in the wind. After the wind came an earthquake. But Yahweh was not in the earthquake. After the earthquake came a fire. But Yahweh was not in the fire. And after the fire there came the sound of a gentle breeze. And when Elijah heard this, he covered his face with his cloak . . .' (1 K 19:11–13).

It is hard to understand God's might, which is manifested more strongly in love than in external force. Yet this love is not weakness, but a power to change men and alter the world. It is the Spirit of God who filled Jesus and with whom Jesus wishes to 'baptise' men. We cannot understand it unless we ourselves are grasped and moved by this Spirit of Love. The Baptist's words to Israel in Jn 1:26 are valid for Christians too: 'There stands among you [one who is] unknown to you.'

The Mission of Jesus

Mk 1: 35–38

In the morning, long before dawn, he got up and left the house, and went off to a lonely place and prayed there. Simon and his companions set out in search of him, and when they found him they said, 'Everybody is looking for you.' He answered, 'Let us go elsewhere, to the neighbouring country towns, so that I can preach there too, because that is why I came.'

This scene, which concludes an initial ministry in Capernaum, has been described for us by Mark. The previous evening, so the evangelist tells us, the inhabitants of the little town brought all their sick and possessed to Simon Peter's house, where Jesus had that afternoon cured Peter's mother-in-law of a fever. 'The whole town came crowding round the door.' Jesus healed many of the diseased and afflicted, and cast out unclean spirits from the possessed. The darkness and wretchedness of human existence was particularly evident in these poor individuals, and when Jesus cured them, the crowd felt some of the liberating power which came out of him. Yet on the following morning Jesus avoided the crowds by slipping off very early, and then made for a lonely place.

What he is looking for in that lonely place is not just peace and quiet in which to rest a while. Despite the few words with which Mark described the scene, he leaves no doubt as to its meaning: Jesus is reflecting on the purpose of his public ministry, on the mission which he knows to be his. The evangelist says succinctly but significantly: 'And [he] prayed there'. In communion with God, Jesus rediscovers his resolve to persevere beyond the first scenes of successful ministry. The reader can readily surmise that Jesus is not thinking his own thoughts and desires, but is searching for the will of Another. Having submitted himself totally to God, his sole concern from then on is to carry out God's will for him. The baptism of Jesus and the forty days in the desert which followed it (1 : 10–13) prepare us for this characteristic of Jesus's life : he is God's beloved Son on whom his favour rests and to whom he imparts the fulness of his Spirit. Jesus is indeed 'driven' by the Spirit of God, driven out into the wilderness. There he is tempted by Satan, but remains steadfast in his communion with God. The 'lonely place' of his prayer recalls the desert (the verbal imagery is very similar in Greek), even though the desert has other connotations besides. But common to both scenes is seclusion from men and nearness to God. Mark gives his readers no clue to the content of Jesus's prayer; it is enough that they can recognise the mystery from which Jesus sustains his life, the hidden strength behind everything he does. There is no trace of a psychological or pietist description.

Are we meant to think of a temptation Jesus avoided from the constant crowds and the apparent success of his ministry? The idea is not out of place, because the disciples who had gone after him said, 'Everybody is looking for you.' Jesus's answer, 'Let us go elsewhere, to the neighbouring country towns,' reads almost like a refusal in the face of an enticing invitation. Mark does not tell us what Satan's temptations of Christ involved (1 : 13). We learn more about them only from Matthew's and Luke's fuller account. This, however, betrays the reflections and particular intentions of the Jewish Christian circles in which the more detailed version arose, and for Mark it is not absolutely necessary. There is another scene in Mark's Gospel in which Peter is tempted to deflect Jesus from his course. When Jesus first informed the disciples of his need to suffer and die, Peter, as usual spokesman for the disciples, spoke up and contradicted him. Jesus rebuked him: 'Get behind me, Satan! Because the way you think is not God's way but man's' (8 : 33). It is not therefore illogical to suppose that in the temptations in the desert too, Mark was thinking of the customary picture of an earthly, political Messiah and the temptation to worldly power and position while God had destined his Chosen One to quite another path. From the very beginning of his Gospel, though not always overtly, Mark has Jesus's way of the Cross in mind, and his purpose is to show his readers that it was all in God's plan so that they too many be encouraged to follow it (cf. 8 : 34–38). It is enough to have shown once that Jesus is obedient to God's mission for him.

Jesus has already begun his public ministry, an extensive activity among the people, especially in Galilee round Lake Gennesaret. But his decisive mission is not to cure and work wonders, but to announce as widely as possible the Good News of God's approaching Kingdom (1:15). Jesus has started to proclaim this; the cures and casting out of demons are designed only to support his message by symbolising the coming of the Kingdom and the defeat of Satan. And so Jesus invites his disciples to leave Capernaum and to go into the outlying villages. The change which Jesus wishes to bring about is not the abolition of all pain and hardship, but primarily men's change of heart, their 'conversion' (1:15; cf. 6:12). His miracles are only signs that God is ready and willing to put an end to material need, too, and to fulfil his promises.

In this presentation of Mark, something about Jesus's true spirit strikes us. He looks on men not to offer them cheap material help, but to nourish them in their deepest humanity. Man has first to be freed from his own inner estrangement; the freedom and love of God's Kingdom must first be disclosed. Only men who are free in themselves can administer freedom profitably to others. It is certainly true that Jesus does not limit the salvation he brings to an inner realm of soul; the Kingdom of God whose herald he is and which is already visible in his works, is a kingdom of total, all-encompassing happiness and joy. Jesus wants to lead men to put love into practice here and now, to see their neighbour's need, to do away with injustice and oppression, to share their earthly goods with one another, to improve existing conditions. But he knows that to achieve this a change of conscience is necessary, that really effective and long-lasting measures stem from a man's heart. Men will transform the world as we know it only when they have themselves been transformed by God's love. Will they be successful? Is it not rather a utopian undertaking to transform man? But it is Jesus himself who sets this movement in motion, and calls other men to follow him. He is urged on by this thought. The community who hear him must take up the Good News, propagate it and carry his words all over the world.

Conquering Fear

Mk 4: 36–41

Leaving the crowd behind they took him, just as he was, in the boat; and there were other boats with him. Then it began to blow a gale and the waves were breaking into the boat so that it was almost swamped. But he was in the stern, his head on the cushion, asleep. They woke him and said to him, 'Master, do you not care? We are going down!' And he woke up and rebuked the wind and said to the sea, 'Quiet now! Be calm!' And the wind dropped, and all was calm again. Then he said to them, 'Why are you so frightened? How is it that you have no faith?' They were filled with awe and said to one another, 'Who can this be? Even the wind and the sea obey him.'

In the primitive Church, this story was the great lesson of overcoming discouragement and fear. The reproof to the disciples is addressed equally to later believers: 'Why are you so frightened? How is it that you have no faith?' The disciples' conduct in the storm at sea shows up their fear and cowardice. Their near-panic is in sharp contrast to Jesus's calm: he is asleep on a cushion, ignoring the wind and the waves. Jesus is the image of quiet confidence. It is possible that this was the original point of the story. In the cursing and withering of the fig-tree, Jesus urged his disciples to 'have faith in God' (11:22), and the final saying about faith that can move mountains confirmed it: the disciples must strive for the energy and vitality of a confidence rooted personally in God. But then the end of the story about the storm turns the reader's attention in another direction: to Jesus, the Lord of wind and waves. Another type of 'fear' is spoken of at this point: the disciples were filled with awe at the power of one whom even the wind and the sea obeyed. The point of the story thus shifts slightly, but without jolting the reader's attention. The disciples are made dramatically aware of God's might and power in Jesus. But there is still a tension between Jesus's words about putting fear behind them and the concluding verse which speaks of a great fear as a holy awe.

Let us return a moment to the description of the storm and the disciples' behaviour. Humanly speaking, their excitement is understandable. The difficulty they are in on the lake takes them by surprise with its elemental force and increasing danger. The storm throws water into the boat, and in no time at all they fear they are about to sink. The fury of the storm is purposely described as if it were the unleashing of demonic forces. Then we are told that Jesus commanded the winds and the sea: 'Quiet now! Be calm!' For the men of that time storms at sea and shipwreck were among the most terrible of human experiences; men

43

felt exposed and impotent in the face of such mighty forces. The same imagery appears frequently in the Old Testament; flooding and waves were symbols of suffering and mortal peril. 'Deep is calling to deep as your cataracts roar; all your waves, your breakers, have rolled over me' (Ps 42:7). Yet the faithful Israelite trusts in God: 'That is why each of your servants prays to you in time of trouble; even if floods come rushing down, they will never reach him' (Ps 32:6). In controlling the storm and the waves, God manifests his might: 'You calm the clamour of the ocean, the clamour of its waves' (Ps 65:7).

In one of the Psalms there is even a passage which reads very much like Jesus's calming of the storm:

> He spoke and raised a gale,
> lashing up towering waves.
> Flung to the sky, then plunged to the depths,
> they lost their nerve in the ordeal,
> staggering and reeling like drunkards
> with all their seamanship adrift.
>
> Then they called to Yahweh in their trouble
> and he rescued them from their sufferings,
> reducing the storm to a whisper
> until the waves grew quiet.
>
> Ps 107:25–29

Despite the similarity here, Mark's account has a different flavour; its most dramatic feature is the contrast between the Master and his terrified disciples. The disciples woke Jesus up and reproached him: 'Do you

44

not care? We are going down!' This was naked fear, without a trace of courage or trust. This is precisely the reproach that Jesus makes to his disciples.

There is another relevant scene, this time Jesus's own terrible fear of death in the Garden of Gethsemane. 'A sudden fear came over him, and great distress' (14:34); but he prays to his Father, and this simple call, unique in Mark's Gospel, expresses his trust even in the bitter anticipation of death. He prays that the cup might be taken away from him, but he adds: 'Let it be as you, not I, would have it.' As he acknowledges elsewhere, he knows that he has a cup to drink and a baptism to be baptised with (10:38)—here again we notice the image of the waters of death. So it is permissible to think that in stilling the storm, at least according to one view of the scene, Jesus is contrasted with the disciples as the one who in his trust in God defies the powers of evil. The strength of his trust is seen in his command of the wind and waves.

At the same time, Jesus's power over the sudden storm prompts the reader to think more about the authority delegated to him. The disciples stand in awe at some sense of mystery surrounding the person of Jesus. In their question 'Who can this be? Even the wind and the sea obey him,' we can glimpse the faith of the community. For Mark, Jesus's authority, which is visible equally in cures and the casting out of devils, is a 'secret epiphany' of the Son of God. Both aspects are compatible with Mark's way of thinking: Jesus the model of believing trust in God and the wonderworker relying on divine power. This man who has an unheard-of strength of trust is also possessed of God's authority, he stands in unique closeness to God, he is God's Son.

In belief in him the community find their trust in God; for in the story of Jesus they experience God's hidden power to avert evil and even to conquer death itself.

Jesus's Authority and the Crisis of Authority Today

Many of the younger generation today, in their criticisms of the Church, appeal to Jesus in his vehement attack on the nation's authorities at the time and in his censure of the incompetent officials who abused their position. It is true that Jesus seems to have distinguished himself by his outspoken criticisms of authority. But it must not be overlooked that in the Gospels as we have them a lot must be ascribed to the evangelists. They were waging an active anti-Jewish polemic, aimed principally at the Pharisees who after the Jewish War and the destruction of Jerusalem succeeded to the exclusive leadership of Judaism and began a fierce campaign against apostates with reprisals against the Christian communities. This said, enough remains, and more, to justify our referring to Jesus's criticisms of conditions in his time and of the behaviour of the Jewish ruling circles. The parable of the Good Samaritan (Lk 10:30–37) refers somewhat provocatively to a priest and a Levite, who—perhaps on their way to minister in the temple—passed by on the other side without going to the aid of the wounded traveller. In the teaching about cleanness and uncleanness, Jesus takes

47

a concrete example which clearly holds up to ridicule the rabbinic interpretation of the Law. By means of a vow, people were able to avoid supporting their parents in their old age (Mt 7:11–12). Jesus seems frequently to have countered too narrow an understanding of what was forbidden on the sabbath. He also took exception to many displays of piety, such as the self-complacency pilloried in the parable of the Pharisee and the publican (Lk 18:10–14). Although not all Pharisees were like this—many of them were genuinely pious and had a sincere regard for their neighbour—the failings of many of these so-called models of piety were sufficient to occasion severe criticism from Jesus, just such as the prophets of old had expressed in the name of their God.

Jesus demanded a mentality and a conduct, based on an uncompromising decision, in which the love of God would be paramount, and this demand he made with unique authority. This is mentioned so often in the Gospels that there can be no doubt about it. His opponents repeatedly challenged Jesus's authority, accusing him of blasphemy when he forgave a poor cripple his sins (Mk 2:3–8), demanding a sign from heaven on another occasion so that he could prove his credentials for the way he spoke and acted (Mk 8:11, 29–30 and par.). There is a particular pericope in which the question of Jesus's authority was raised in a dispute with representatives of the ruling Jews. It comes immediately after the cleansing of the temple, an action on Jesus's part whose precise significance is disputed but which was most definitely an act of extreme provocation (Mk 11:27–33 and par.). This passage deserves our closest attention because it juxtaposes Jesus's authority and official Jewish authority, distinguishing true from false.

The question of authority probably goes with Jesus's attack on the traders and money-changers in the temple forecourt. In Mark and to some extent in John (2: 13–22) this can still be seen. In holy zeal for God's house (cf. Jn 2:17), Jesus dared to demonstrate opposition to a practice permitted by all the temple officials. In their view the tolerance of this traffic was eminently reasonable as it facilitated the regulations laid down for lawful worship. The temple dues payable once a year by every Jew had to be discharged in old money, and for this money-changers were necessary; the sacrifices prescribed for a variety of occasions required the statutory sacrificial animals (doves) needed to be readily available to frequenters of the temple. For what reason should permission be denied the traders to carry on these honest dealings in the forecourt? Jesus simply sweeps such human considerations aside, and enacts a prophetic sign. Zeal for God's affairs was nothing new in Israel; side by side with institutional religion, the Jews had always had a prophetic element among them, urging passionate commitment to true and inner service to God. In the Synoptic account, there is a quotation from the book of Jeremiah: 'You have turned [my house] into a robbers' den' (Mk 11:17). This establishes a conflict between the official guardians of cult and Jesus's prophetic zeal. What presumption is this? What right has Jesus to defy the Jewish leaders whose word was decisive in all questions of law and temple worship?

In the dispute over Jesus's authority, this episode is of fundamental importance. The Jewish leaders call on

Jesus to state without equivocation by what authority he acts or who gave him the authority. These official Jewish representatives suspect Jesus's claim, and they demand some form of ratification. As Jews, they could not altogether exclude the possibility of a prophet; but whoever could not substantiate a claim to act like this in God's name was obviously a false prophet, and legal proceedings would have to be taken. They knew that they themselves were the holders of proper, God-given authority. God gave his people the Law of Moses on Sinai, and these teachers of the Law and leaders of the people were conscious of being its official guardians and interpreters. It is, if one likes, a conflict between institution and charism, legal order and prophetic mission, and the former can challenge the latter to produce its credentials.

Jesus puts the elders a counter-question, prefacing it with the remark that he will tell them what they wish to know if they can answer it. He does not essentially contest the authority of the Jewish leaders, but queries the way in which they understand and exercise it. His question concerns John the Baptist: was his baptism from God or man, that is, was his prophetic ministry, demand for inner conversion and baptism for repentance willed by God or not? This question rather embarrassed the Jewish leaders. They had not joined the crowds who flocked to hear the voice of one crying in the wilderness. They had listened to John, perhaps examined him too (cf. Jn 1:19–28), but they had neither believed him nor submitted to his baptism (cf. Mt 21:32). Yet they could not say anything publicly against the prophetic mission of so popular a preacher. Either they were unable, or against their better judgement unwilling, to come to a decision which would entail so many personal consequences from the Baptist's invitation to repent. This is what Jesus wishes to expose: their alleged authority failed when an obvious decision was to be made, and when personal consequences were demanded. Their leadership is not convincing, their authority is outward only; in the conceit of their hearts they claim what is not in fact theirs.

The evangelist relates how the elders put their heads together to decide what answer they should give. If they said that John's baptism was from God, they risked being asked by Jesus why they did not then believe him. If, on the other hand, they replied that it was from man, not God-willed at all, and that John had not been sent by God as a prophet, they would have to reckon with the fury of the people who accepted John as a true prophet. They would dearly like to have disputed the Baptist's divine calling, but because of the people they lacked the courage to do it. Fearing for their authority, they shrewdly maintained silence. Even if this scene owes a lot to the imagination of the evangelist (these representatives of the Jewish authorities dared not express their own thoughts in public), their reactions as described do reflect what any person would do who compulsively clings to external authority and attempts to defend it. Their shameful silence amounts to a cowardly retreat.

Jesus's attitude would be misjudged if his counterquestion were to be regarded simply as a clever gambit. He wanted to force his opponents to speak out. The question of John the Baptist, whom Jesus himself acknowledged to be a great prophet (cf. Mt 11:9–10), suited his purpose admirably. Their attitude towards this exceptional man and his call to conversion would show whether these leaders of Judaism were willing and able to recognise God's hand even when it was uncomfortable for them. Even John had no other proof for his mission and authority than his own word and the witness of his life which clearly demonstrated to those prepared to take it that God's authority was behind him. In this connection Jesus is in much the same situation as John: he, too, has no external evidence for the legitimacy of his ministry. The leaders refused to acknowledge his miracles of healing, but asked instead for a special sign from heaven. Even less were they ready to accept his message of God's merciful love to all men, even the socially contemptible and under-privileged, as it was preached by Jesus and demonstrated in his own pattern of living. They no more thought of bowing to this than they did to John's preaching. And so Jesus asked them for their considered opinion on John's baptism. 'If they could come to no decision on the Baptist's prophetic authority, then they need expect no pronouncement on the source of Jesus's authority' (J. Roloff).

What, however, is Jesus's authority precisely? The reference back to the ministry of John the Baptist does not allow us to draw the conclusion that Jesus understood his own mission as entirely comparable. The relevant parable of the children playing in the market place (Mt 11:16–19 and Lk 7:31–35), preserved for us in an old tradition, makes it clear that in his own mind his work was essentially different from John's: John was an austere man of repentance, while the 'Son of Man' was not loath to share the joys of a banquet, fraternised almost ostentatiously with 'tax collectors and sinners', and enjoyed ill-repute as the friend of these social outcasts. Also the content of Jesus's message was different, although one thing at least he had in common with John: he knew that his special mission came from God, that he had been sent on work reserved for him. Thus both belonged to the long line of God's prophets, chosen by God for his service, responsible to him alone, and accredited by him alone. If the Pharisees and elders had answered Jesus's question by accepting the divine provenance of John's baptism, Jesus would most probably have given them the same answer with regard to his own authority: my authority too is from God, my doings are backed by his brief and authorisation. This is an unheard-of claim, made with direct and unmistakable certainty and leading ultimately to the mystery of Jesus's person. This, too, must be remembered, if one is not to draw false conclusions from Jesus's attitudes and his conflict with the 'official' authority (God-given, according to the Jewish mentality) of the temple ministers, the scribes and the elders.

What are the correspondences of Jesus's clash with the Jewish leaders with our modern problems of authority, commitment and freedom, criticism of authority and anti-authoritarian attitudes? We can certainly say that legitimate authority must still prove itself, not only by external things (the possession of power, the existing institution, legally-assumed office), but also by an inner power of conviction, a genuine 'authority', a just use of the institution, and an exercise of office that serves the common good. It is far more difficult to decide when the holder of an office has lost his authority, must step down or should be deposed. There must always be a certain elasticity to allow for human weakness and failure. Jesus made no attempt to incite the people against their leaders, who after all were failing in matters of prime importance, and to topple them. On the other hand he did speak out so clearly and so sharply against them that their authority was shaken. He even rejected them as religious leaders of Judaism. True to the conviction of his divine mission, he left the practical consequences to God, or as we might say, to the course of human history in which God's plans for him unfolded. Whether, and if so how far, he would have agreed to an overthrow by force of unjust rulers and brutal regimes is a question that cannot be reliably answered from the Gospel texts.

In our pericope, anyway, it is not political but 'spiritual' authority that is at stake, and by that is meant any human exercise of leadership in God's name. This is the most difficult question of all: who has the right and authority to undertake such leadership, and who the right to criticise and even perhaps depose? In concrete terms, what is the position of spiritual authority in the Church, who has the right to criticise the holders of ecclesiastical office, and who can be called on to administer the sometimes necessary correction to 'official' actions? If the Church is to be truly the Church of Jesus Christ, there is only one true and final source of authority, and that is Jesus Christ himself. It was founded by his authority, and is governed by his word and will. Its office-holders must prove their worth to him, and give him an account of whether and how well they exercise their ministry in the service of the Church and mankind: in loyalty to the Gospel and its demands, or in self-seeking and compliance with human weakness and cowardice. From the very beginning, the Church has had its 'official' ministers, its institution, and side by side with that, freely-given charismatic ministries, the prophetic element. If a member of the Church feels himself called to a charismatic or prophetic role, he must ask himself very seriously whether he is acting with divine endorsement, in fulfilment of Christ's authority, and in harmony with the Gospel. Whoever in the Church opposes the Spirit and will of Jesus—or his word as handed down in the Gospels and his intentions as manifest in his actions—loses not only his credibility but also the authority which accrues to him through Jesus's power. All genuine Christian authority is exercised with the sole aim of making disciples of men (Mt 28:19) and of carrying on God's, Jesus's, work in the service of mankind. And only he who can convincingly, in his criticisms and demands, call on Jesus and his Gospel, should raise his voice to confront the abuse of human authority in the Church with the authority of Jesus, based on his power as Lord.

Dialogue with Unbelievers—
A Sermon to Theologians

Jn 8: 21–29 (NEB)

Again he said to them, 'I am going away. You will look for me, but you will die in your sin; where I am going you cannot come'. The Jews then said, 'Perhaps he will kill himself: is that what he means when he says, "Where I am going you cannot come"?' So Jesus continued, 'You belong to this world below, I to the world above. Your home is in this world, mine is not. That is why I told you that you would die in your sins. If you do not believe that I am what I am, you will die in your sins'. They asked him, 'Who are you?' Jesus answered, 'Why should I speak to you at all? I have much to say about you—and in judgement. But he who sent me speaks the truth, and what I heard from him I report to the world.'

They did not understand that he was speaking to them about the Father. So Jesus said to them, 'When you have lifted up the Son of Man you will know that I am what I am. I do nothing on my own authority, but in all that I say, I have been taught by my Father. He

*who sent me is present with me, and has not left me
alone; for I always do what is acceptable to him.'*

This text from John's Gospel leads us to think for a
moment about the question of dialogue with unbelievers. Our purpose here and now is not to examine the
content of Jesus's words—it is not an easy text to in-
terpret satisfactorily—but simply to take a brief look at
the thrust and parry of the conversation, at the way in
which Jesus conducts this debate with the Jews. We too
today have to engage in dialogue with the unbelieving,
with people who categorically deny the existence of
God and oppose the Church, and with people also who
have become estranged from the Christian faith and
have dropped out of Church life.

The very fact that a conversation with unbelievers is
reported in this Gospel is noteworthy. Most of Jesus's
words in John are aimed at opponents, at obstinate,
malicious antagonists. They betray the bitter controversies between Jews and Christians at the time John
was writing. Even if our present text is not a record from
the time of Jesus, is not an actual verbal debate taken
down as it happened, it is still evidence for the clash of
John's community with the Jews who were causing so
much trouble. The arguments are theological, central
to the Christian faith, indeed among the most important of all because they concern Jesus's self-witness.

In the dialogue reported in our Gospel reading,
there is a point reached where the conversation threatens to break up altogether. When Jesus is talking about
his going away, the Jews respond with sarcasm:

'Perhaps he will kill himself: is that what he means?' In Judaism, suicide was a grave crime against the Lord of life. Jesus reacts firmly but calmly. Their thoughts are not his, they belong to this world below, caught up in a purely human, earthly mentality. He belongs to the world above, that is, to the realm of God, he knows God and carries out his command. Fearlessly Jesus reminds them of their sins and warns them that they will die in them, that is, that God will reject them. But he does not close all paths to them; one remains open: if they believe in Jesus and his claim, they will escape this fate. The Jews, however, oppose him with even less understanding than before, and Jesus is almost ready to break off the conversation: 'Why should I speak to you at all?' His obstinate interlocutors remain silent. But even then Jesus has not said his last word. Towards the end, when he is talking about being lifted up, he opens new perspectives: 'You will know that I am what I am.' The exact meaning here is disputed, but it seems he is offering them one last chance of salvation. If they refuse to be convinced by his words, then perhaps his obedience to death and his attestation by God will open their eyes. The evangelist is thinking of the Scripture which he adds after the piercing with the lance in a later chapter: 'They shall look on him whom they pierced' (19:37).

What can we learn from this for our own dialogue with unbelievers? At least this: that we must not close all roads. Even when dialogue fails, we know that God can move men's hearts and awaken new faith in them. In conversations like this, the rational argument can never be the last word; we shall not easily bring our opponents to their knees with logical reasoning. Belief in Jesus Christ as the saving ground of our existence demands a total decision to which reason contributes only a part. Reason is often only a cause of contention and a stumbling-block. The life and death of Jesus, on the other hand, is something so moving, the influence of the crucified carpenter's son so profound and powerful, that men, oppressed by the misery of their own existence, will find in him the anchor of their lives. 'They shall look on him whom they pierced.'

In this conversation with his opponents, Jesus displays a surprising severity and inflexibility. The lesson we can draw from this is that we shall never convince unbelievers by accommodating our message to the spirit of the times or by putting up pseudo-scientific camouflage. Theology has deserted its post if it sees its function as a satellite of profane science, whether it be sociology, anthropology, psychology or even humanitarian ethics. In the area of human sciences, we, like philosophers in their own way, if philosophy is to be more that just a handmaid to other sciences, have to enquire into a profundity of human existence which none of these others can reach with the means at their disposal. For us, too, it is a question of concrete experience, but from a point of view that is not scientifically controllable: we look at man as himself a questionable reality, a being at war with himself and never completely himself. Must we, in our attempt to be thoroughly modern, learn from a sociologist what an impossible role the theologian's is? In his remarkable book *A Rumour of Angels*, Peter L. Berger says among other things: 'Logically enough, notions such as "autonomy", "man come of age", and even "democratic humanism" came to be substituted for the earlier expressions of existential anguish. Indeed, if one looks at all this with a little detachment, one is strongly reminded of the children's game of rapidly changing grimaces' (p. 69). In fact, if we as Christian theologians no longer speak about what faith in God means for man, if we no longer have the courage to proclaim Jesus Christ as God's definitive promise to us and the ground of our hope, we are no better than children rapidly changing grimaces, and nobody takes those seriously. Even when we are in dialogue with modern 'atheists', who behave like unbelievers but inwardly thirst for a faith, we shall be accepted only if we stick to our own primitive and essential brief, which is to pose the question of the meaning of human existence and confront 'autonomous' man with the question of God. 'They did not understand that he was speaking to them about the Father.' This same God Jesus speaks about we too must proclaim to our contemporaries; Jesus has shown us the way to bring the distant and alien God nearer to us once more.

All right, like Jesus's, our words too often bear no fruit. But there comes a time in the life of every man when, tired of life and disillusioned, he ponders the meaning of his being. Then we should look on him whom they pierced, God's landmark for straying mankind. And when we ourselves are deeply depressed by the unconcern and even enmity of men towards the Christian faith, we should console ourselves with the words Jesus used towards the end of our reading: 'He who sent me is present with me, and has not left me alone.' Elsewhere Jesus said to his disciples: 'If the world hates you, it hated me first, as you know well. . . . Remember what I said: "A servant is not greater than his master"' (15:18 and 20). For the Christian there can never be a situation in which hope fades entirely, because he knows that the Jesus who was lifted up on the Cross is also the Jesus who was raised by God to glory.

Can the Faith be Proved?

Jn 10: 22–26

It was the time when the feast of Dedication was being celebrated in Jerusalem. It was winter, and Jesus was in the Temple walking up and down in the Portico of Solomon. The Jews gathered round him and said, 'How much longer are you going to keep us in suspense? If you are the Christ, tell us plainly.' Jesus replied:

> *'I have told you, but you do not believe.*
> *The works I do in my Father's name are my*
>   *witness;*
> *but you do not believe,*
> *because you are no sheep of mine.'*

This little episode, which the fourth evangelist inserts here at the time of the feast of Dedication, about three months before Jesus's death, is of fundamental importance. Jesus's conflict with the leaders of Judaism ('the Jews') reveals a deep, in fact impassable, gulf: there can be no agreement between the man who speaks God's word and knows that he has been sent by God (cf. 3:34) and these men who obstinately close their hearts to this message. The point at issue in this case is the possibility of belief and the riddle of unbelief which is troubling the evangelist in his confrontation with the unbelieving Jews (cf. 12:37–43). This has lost none of its relevance today: how can we recognise in Jesus the God-sent Saviour, whose word is of unique significance for all men, in whose person the sense and purpose of our existence are contained, and who can lead us unhesitatingly through the darkness of our earthly pilgrimage?

The Jews gathered round Jesus and pressed him to state openly and plainly whether he was 'the Christ', that is, the promised Saviour. Whatever the expectations bound up with this particular title, the Jews demand a clear and unambiguous statement of who Jesus thinks he is. If he claims to be the Messiah, it is a decisive piece of intelligence on which they could at least take a definite stance. They will not be put off any longer. A justified request, so they think. Jesus's answer is quite simple: 'I have told you,' he states categorically, and then adds, 'but you do not believe me.' If we examine John's Gospel closely, we notice with surprise that nowhere does Jesus publicly state that he *is* the Christ. He reveals his identity only to two individuals, the Samaritan woman (4:26), and the man born blind (9:37). Among the people, especially at the feast of Tabernacles in Jerusalem (chapter 7), there are continual questions and discussions as to whether Jesus is the Messiah or not, but Jesus does not take any direct part in them himself. How, then, can he turn round and answer the Jews that he has told them already? The fourth evangelist knows full well that Jesus never publicly called himself the Messiah, but he also knows that everything Jesus said or did proclaims his messiahship. Jesus manifestly is the Saviour, not of course in the worldly, political sense of a national liberator and 'King of the Jews', as most Jews expected, but in a much deeper and fuller sense.

However, nobody who prejudges Jesus's life and activity, rejecting it out of hand with distrust and scepticism, can see clearly who it is that speaks here. For him Jesus remains an enigma, an obscure phenomenon, and so Jesus adds: 'But you do not believe me.' He follows this with an invitation to consider the works he does in his Father's name, that is, by God's will and power. *They* are his witness, *they* declare who he is and why he has come. Humanly speaking, the actions that can be seen and not doubted are more convincing than mere words that cannot be checked. A little later Jesus says to the same Jews: 'Even if you refuse to believe in [my words], at least believe in the work I do' (10:38).

The final insight we glean from this little episode is the following: there is no purely rational path that gives access to the person of Jesus. We have to bring an open heart ready to embrace the faith if we wish to share his mystery. We can and must meditate on the phenomenon of 'Jesus of Nazareth', but we cannot scientifically locate it and pigeon-hole its various aspects into ready-made categories. There is basis enough for the statement of faith that Jesus is 'the Christ, the Son of God' (20:31); faith is not irrational, but it does exceed reason in the sense of rational demonstration. This faith cannot be proved to someone who does not believe; but if anyone believes and lives according to that belief, he will experience its truth (cf. 7:17–18).

The Believers' Attitude

Jn 10: 27–30

> *The sheep that belong to me listen to my voice;*
> *I know them and they follow me.*
> *I give them eternal life;*
> *they will never be lost*
> *and no one will ever steal them from me.*
> *The Father who gave them to me is greater than*
> *   anyone,*
> *and no one can steal from the Father.*
> *The Father and I are one.*

These words about those who hear Jesus's voice, which are found in his preaching at the feast of Dedication and are formally addressed to unbelieving Jews, are better intended for the ears of believers. Otherwise they could seem slightly strange: it is as if the Shepherd were boasting that the sheep that belong to him listen to his voice, and can never be stolen from him. Does Jesus want to shame the unbelieving? Do believers wish to justify themselves in the word of their Lord and take pride in their own election? No, these words, like the whole Shepherd pericope to which they belong (10: 1–18), are simply intended to strengthen the readers of the Gospel in their faith and join them more closely to their Lord. There is an inseparable bond between Jesus and his faithful disciples, a familiarity, a mutual knowing and loving (cf. 14–15).

Given the historical background, this passage takes on its peculiar meaning in the situation of the Christian community to which John belonged. They are hard pressed by hostile and influential Jews of the same town. They must hold their ground and wage a spiritual war of defence in which they could very easily lose courage and become despondent. The image of the flock assures them that they enjoy the closest bonds of fellowship with Christ and with each other. As regards the attacks on them from outsiders, it tells them that they are safe in Jesus and his Father.

In a hard-pressed situation such as this, there is always the danger of introspection, of shutting oneself off from outside influences. It has been said in fact of the Johannine community that it was a group on the fringe, suffering from a sectarian complex and in danger of turning itself into a ghetto. However, if one looks more closely, the Johannine community certainly did not cut themselves off as a sect would, and they did not write off their unbelieving fellow-citizens as hopelessly lost. As well as the rather harsh words of polemic, John's Gospel also gives us plenty of gentleness. For example; even at a time when the refusal of the Jewish leaders and the people's lack of understanding must have seemed to be irredeemably fixed, Jesus cried out in public: 'While you still have the light, believe in the light and you will become sons of light' (12:36). Although Jesus's disciples do not 'belong to the world', yet they are sent 'into the world' (17:14 and 18).

Our situation today is very similar to the Johannine community's of that time: many believers feel they are under attack, forced into defensive positions, and so are often unsure of themselves. This suggests that they have closed themselves off with the like-minded, holding even the unlike-minded in the same Church at a distance. Too many of the faithful, in their view, fraternise excessively with contemporary society and come very near to conforming to it. No one can deny such Christians the right to appeal to Jesus's words as recalled above. It does all of us good to be made aware of our calling, of our fellowship with Christ, of our security in God. But at the same time there is a danger of looking down on others and of holding outsiders at arm's length without due consideration of all the facts. Do we really know whom God has chosen, who are those on whom the Good Shepherd has lavished the life won for a fallen world by his life, death and resurrection? Elsewhere our evangelist says that Jesus died 'to gather together in unity the scattered children of God' (11:52). Who are these scattered, rather anonymous, children of God? Only a Christianity aware, with an immovable certainty of faith, of its mission in the world, of its duty to offer salvation to all men, is healthy, and imitates Jesus's example to go out and search for the lost sheep.

Jesus's words in John's Gospel lead us to the very heart of the faith. The Johannine Jesus, the Christ of our faith, can speak in no other way than this because he knows he is one with the Father and that it is from the Father that he received notice of what to say and what to do (cf. 12:50). Those who believe in him have no choice but to acknowledge that they are the salvific community who through the Son of God, whom they have known and experienced, receive life. But to speculate on who belongs to the elect, the predestined, is dangerous; such questions impinge upon the secrecy of God. Election rightly understood confers humility and kindliness—humility, because it is due to no merit of our own if we enjoy a lucid and steady faith; kindliness, because we know that God wills all men to be saved and yet see that many still need to achieve belief. He who has experienced faith as the light and pole-star of human life can only wish that all men might see this light, and in their darkness and uncertainty search it out.

A Proof from Scripture

Jn 10: 32–38

Jesus said to them, 'I have done many good works for you to see, works from my Father; for which of these are you stoning me?' The Jews answered him, 'We are not stoning you for doing a good work but for blasphemy: you are only a man and you claim to be God'. Jesus answered:

'Is it not written in your Law:
I said, you are gods?
So the Law uses the word gods
of those to whom the word of God was addressed,
and scripture cannot be rejected.
Yet you say to someone the Father has conse-
  crated and sent into the world,
"You are blaspheming",
because he says, "I am the Son of God".
If I am not doing my Father's work,
there is no need to believe me;
but if I am doing it,
then even if you refuse to believe in me,
at least believe in the work I do;
then you will know for sure
that the Father is in me and I am in the Father.'

In the discussion between the unbelieving Jews, who refuse to be convinced by Jesus's works, and Jesus, who will not waive his claim to be the Saviour sent into the world by God his Father, we are given a rather curious proof from Scripture. It is taken from one of the Psalms in which unjust judges are called 'gods' (Ps 82: 6). God the supreme judge will call them to account; they shall die like other men. The original sense, therefore, squares badly with the train of thought in this passage from John's Gospel. Here the reasoning is roughly as follows: if Scripture does not disdain to call 'gods' those to whom God's word had been addressed, then *a fortiori* the Man who has brought God's definitive word of salvation deserves the title 'Son of God'. This kind of scriptural proof, which depends entirely on a particular wording, is typical of Jewish scribes at the time of the evangelist, and there is no doubt that the passage is directed specifically at them. In no other place in the New Testament do we find any similar argument from this psalm. So we must look again at the discussion of the Johannine community with contemporary Jewry.

The evangelist has deliberately shaped Jesus's words to give them the maximum effect on the unbelieving Jews in his own city. If we are looking for an exact 'historical' account this might well put us off, but we know that the conviction that Jesus was the Messiah and the Son of God did not depend in the Christian mentality on this proof from Scripture. Their faith has a different basis altogether which we can also detect in this passage.

Jesus cites all the works which he performed publicly in the sight of the Jews. They come from the

Father, indeed they are the Father's works. The evangelist is certainly thinking of the series of miracles which he calls 'signs': the cures related in chapters 4 and 5, the feeding of the five thousand in chapter 6, the healing of the man born blind in chapter 9. They each reveal something about the deepest salvific significance of Jesus: the giver of life, the true bread from heaven, the light of the world. If we understand this correctly, the miracles ('signs') are not related for their power to astonish and impress, but rather to draw attention to various aspects of the person of Jesus. In fact the words and explanations of Jesus are at least equally significant; the signs are merely 'enacted revelations'. Ultimately it is Jesus's whole 'work', everything he has said, done and suffered on earth, that proves he is the one sent by God (cf. 17:4). His resurrection, which the evangelist sees as his 'exaltation' by the Father, sets the divine seal on it all.

It is on these grounds that the Johannine community believed Jesus to be the Messiah and the Son of God. But to make this belief of theirs more acceptable to their contemporaries, especially their Jewish neighbours, they used a variety of arguments more likely to carry weight. 'Believe in the works' of Jesus even if you do not believe in him or his words! He is in total communion with God, God has spoken and acted through him.

We, too, must give witness to the world we live in of our belief in Jesus Christ, and be ready to give an account of it in terms that are intelligible today. We can no longer use the kind of scriptural proof that John offers to the unbelieving Jewish scribes of his own day. But the person and work of Jesus are still valid, and in an interpretation which takes the modern horizon of understanding into account, they will achieve a heightened significance. For the men of our time we must present the whole personality of the earthly, historical Jesus more powerfully than ever: his love for sinners, his concern for the poor and the oppressed, his protest against social abuses and the intolerant attitude of men who want to appear pious, etc. In this respect the synoptic Gospels are more readily acceptable; but we could not do without that deeper reflection on the person of Jesus such as we find in John's Gospel. For only this view of the faith can give us an ultimate answer to the otherwise impenetrable mystery of Jesus of Nazareth.

The Challenge of the Easter Message

It would be quite wrong to think that the Easter message, 'Jesus who was crucified has risen', makes impossible demands on modern man's credulity. It has always been a challenge to human reason from the very beginnings of Christianity. Those who first heard it had problems that were different from ours, certainly, but probably no easier to live with. We should not delude ourselves that we can understand it better by explaining most of it away or removing everything that might be a scandal to our modern imagination.

What, then, was the situation in Judaism when the great news of Jesus's resurrection was first formulated and proclaimed from the housetops? The Jews in general believed in the resurrection of the dead at the end of time, in a future world. When Jesus lived, most of them acknowledged such a belief, but not all of them. For example, the influential party of the Sadducees, among whom were numbered many conservative (especially high priestly) circles, rejected it. Whether the Essenes, about whom we know so much more since the discovery of the Qumran texts, accepted it is still disputed, because despite the richness of the Qumran literature, there is nothing explicit about an after-life.

73

But, many will object, it is perfectly clear that belief in a resurrection from the dead was widespread at the time. So, you see, already there is a massive gap between ourselves and the period in question. Those people had a completely different world-view which we with our sophisticated scientific advances have long surpassed. They experienced no difficulty in imagining that the dead could take on new flesh and be raised to life again. For us, though, it is quite ludicrous and fantastic to think that the millions and millions of men who have ever lived on earth could emerge from their graves. They have all long since turned to dust and ashes, been changed into other substances and then recycled into the earth's organic processes.

However, belief in the resurrection is not nearly, of course, so easily disposed of as that. Men of Jesus's time, too, raised objections to it, although with other arguments. The Sadducees, for example, attempted to show how absurd the Pharisees' belief in resurrection was. The Gospels record an occasion on which they tried to trap Jesus with a question on it: what happens when a woman takes a husband, then after his death marries his brother, and so on for seven brothers? Whose wife will she be at the resurrection? Jesus answered the question quite seriously: you understand neither the Scriptures nor the power of God. When they rise from the dead, men and women do not marry. God is a God of the living, and his position as the God of Israelite fathers who were long dead proves it (cf. Mk 12:18–27). This reply of Jesus says something extremely important: resurrection is not return to earthly life, it gives access to a life utterly different from our present one and quite beyond the reach of our experience.

It is the goal and completion of human living and human history, as inaccessible to investigation as the origin of the world, attainable only in faith.

Another point about Judaism must be made here: despite their belief in the future resurrection, it was un-heard-of for a person who had died in the sight of hundreds still living, so quickly to achieve resurrection. They believed in the resurrection of the just or even of all men at the end of time, yes; but they could never conceive the possibility of an individual's reaching life's fulfilment already. It is precisely this, though, that Jesus's disciples intended to affirm when they announced that Jesus, who had been crucified, was risen from the dead. The reader will not be deceived by the differences in the presentations of the evangelists which express the reality of Jesus's resurrection and the identity of the risen with the crucified Jesus by using rather crude examples (the risen Lord ate with his disciples, showed them his wounds, could be touched). What the Easter accounts all have in common is that the disciples experienced Jesus as being quite different, as no longer a part of earthly reality. What they wished to express with their Easter message was this: Jesus, who was rejected and killed by men, is justified and attested by God, and has become a sign of the world to come. He himself has entered this new life, and invites all who believe in him to follow him there. He is the pledge of their life's hope, the 'first-fruits of all who have fallen asleep' (cf. 1 Co 15:20–23), the 'prince of life' (Ac 3:15). In the context of contemporary Judaism, this was a novelty of astonishing boldness.

And what was the situation in the Greek world to which the early Christian missionaries next carried their tidings of the crucified and risen Jesus? For them the shock was even greater. Any such belief was absolutely nonsensical and grotesque; it contradicted all their traditions of thought. The great Greek philosophers, who had pondered deeply on human existence, certainly taught the immortality of the soul; but the idea that a man could rise up in both body and soul was intolerable. Paul's speech on the Areopagus in Athens is a well-known case in point. The author of Acts writes: 'At this mention of rising from the dead, some of them burst out laughing; others said, "We would like to hear you talk about this again"' (17:32). The Greek thinkers were so convinced of the superiority of mind over matter that they pictured man's perfection as a liberation from the material body, in other words as bodiless happiness. Because of this they had little wish to join in the 'resurrection of the dead'. The Christian message of a crucified man rising again was in defiance of their whole philosophy.

We know that very early on certain elements in Christianity tried to extenuate the doctrine of the resurrection. Gnostics, for example, falsified it by saying that our resurrection has already taken place: we already possess the divine Spirit who raises us here and now in our lifetimes to a higher plane of existence; we have already achieved perfection. The primitive Church rejected this as a misrepresentation: as long as we remain on earth, we are frail imperfect subjects of suffering. The resurrection is only a hope for us, but one that is substantiated because Christ is risen. Paul impressed it on his readers: Jesus was crucified, and on earth we are committed to this crucified Jesus so that we may then rise with him to new life.

Our own difficulties today with the Easter message are different again. It is said that this whole imagery of resurrection is an apocalyptic idea which was all right for the past but is no longer acceptable in the present. When Jesus's disciples claimed that their crucified Lord had risen, they merely wanted to express the fact that even after his death Jesus was with them. They were convinced of his continuing presence when they came together for a common meal just as they had done with Jesus in his lifetime. They experienced him as their mighty Lord still active in their midst, and they were driven to go out in his strength and carry on his work. It is consequently a significant development that later Christians thought less about the earthly Jesus and more about the Lord who was with God, and then worshipped him as a god. Today we have to go back to the earthly Jesus and continue his ministry.

This last suggestion is in many ways justified. If we let the earthly Jesus slip from our thoughts, if we forget his challenging demands and concentrate overmuch on the divine Redeemer, we have not fully grasped the Easter message. That states about the earthly Jesus that he was attested by God and made Lord. The risen Jesus gave his disciples a mission: 'Make disciples of all the nations ... teach them to observe all the commands I gave you' (Mt 28:19–20). In this way the earthly Jesus, now acknowledged as Lord, is more than ever in the community's thoughts; the risen Lord wants us to carry out his work as he did on earth. But in criticism of the new attempts to limit the primitive Christian Easter message to the continuance of Jesus's earthly ministry, let it be stressed most forcefully here: it suppresses that message's challenge and stultifies its content.

77

To reduce the Christian message to a call for brotherhood and social commitment is to deny the Easter event, which in the early Church was the ground of the hope that it proclaimed to the world. If Christianity has nothing else to offer but a humanitarian philosophy and social critique, it is superfluous and dispensable. What it in fact offers is a message of liberation, of salvation, which provides one answer to the otherwise insoluble problems of human existence: what the meaning of life is, how we can retain our personal freedom in a technological society, how we can cope fruitfully with our life even when illness and old age depress us and all we have to look forward to on earth is death. Besides the heavy demands Jesus makes on all who follow him, he also issues an invitation of tremendous warmth and consolation: 'Come to me, all you who labour and are overburdened, and I will give you rest' (Mt 11:28). Besides his realistic view of earthly conditions, there is also his promise: 'Be brave: I have conquered the world' (Jn 16:33). This is and remains the joyful message of our faith trumpeted out in our Easter tidings: the Lord is risen, he is truly risen.

Surely, though, this message is nothing but a verbal intoxicant, a sort of spiritual drug to drown the sorrows of human life? Modern man has become sceptical, he mistrusts empty words and ideologically suspicious talk. He agrees with Friedrich Nietzsche: Christians ought to look more redeemed. This criticism is justified if the faith is reduced to lip-service. But where there are real believers, the force of the ancient message proves itself. It is not a myth about a dying and rising god; it concerns the man Jesus, who lived with us like any other man, but who also lived for us, even to the fearful death on the Cross. Every myth shatters on his suffering and dying. The Easter message is a belief which frees hope for the future. It is not a colourless ideology, because it summoned the disciples to follow, to do, to act for others.

The challenge to reason remains. No attempt to penetrate the Easter appearances scientifically will attain enlightenment or reach a satisfactory conclusion. There were no phenomena which manifested themselves like physical processes in space and time, accessible to all, subject to investigation and experimentally repeatable. There were only events lived out between persons; events experienced by the disciples, with a compulsive certainty that one can share but not prove, as living encounters with their risen Lord.

Men of those times were still receptive to mysteries which baffled the powers of reason. Our time has become so rationalist that it has succumbed to the delusion that reality is exclusively constituted by what can be investigated and proved. Prominent men of science in the past knew the limits of their own knowledge. Blaise Pascal once said, 'The final step of reason is to recognise that there is an infinity of things which surpass it.' It is quite vain to try to clarify rationally the mystery of Jesus's resurrection as it struck the disciples in their experience of the risen Lord. The disciples could say very little about it beyond the fact that Jesus 'appeared' to them in a different way from before, that his closeness kindled their hope: this fulfilment is promised to them, too, and to all who believe in Jesus.

Today philosophers say that what cannot be expressed in language is not a reality that can have any significance for man; that a question to which there is no expressible answer is falsely posed. But does this not betray a rationalism and an agnosticism which put up barriers to man's knowledge which must be overcome if he is in any way to understand the sense of his existence and human history? There are things in the world that cannot be investigated by science, that cannot be grasped by reason and language, and yet are realities. The disciples experienced this in their encounters with the risen Jesus.

Paul calls it the folly of the Cross with which God willed to save a world that could not know him with human wisdom alone (cf. 1 Co 1:21). It is the folly of a faith which, while human reason falters, submits to the power and love of God. We must endeavour to overcome human misery, wherever we meet it, by our love, in accordance with the message of the earthly Jesus. But the ultimate misery of our human existence can be overcome only in the belief that despite failure we are secure in the love of God, despite death we are taken up into his life. This is the unique message of the Christian Easter faith.

Pentecost Then and Now

The event which we refer to as Pentecost or Whitsun was the first Christians' experience of the Spirit of God who comes to dwell in men's hearts and transform their lives. The descent of the Spirit is not an experience that can be achieved by one's own efforts; it is not subject to experimentation or manipulation of any sort. Whoever is fortunate enough to be granted it finds himself moved and overwhelmed by it. The account of the experience in the Acts of the Apostles condenses it into a dramatic episode which, although it owes a great deal to the hand of the author, admirably illustrates the essential qualities of what the disciples and also the community since them have lived through. The sound of a powerful wind and the appearance of tongues of fire are the manifestations of a power which grasps believers almost despite themselves and enables them to do things of which they would have been incapable before: discerning God's dealings, speaking about them, firing others with the same enthusiasm and bringing them all together into living companionship. The result is the first Christian community in Jerusalem, eager to bear witness to the power and love of God which they have experienced, and radiating out into the world

81

around them by the ardour of their faith and the vigour of their fraternal charity.

If we think about this charismatic origin of the Christian life, we see at once what 'Church' really is and should be: not a human organisation with a mass of external apparatus and propaganda, but a union of persons under the invocation of the Holy Spirit, a movement flowing out of the sheer force of their faith and love. Today as well, if we care to look, the Spirit of God manifests himself. Is it not quite astonishing for example how many charismatic figures have emerged in our time, gathered groups of sympathisers round them and initiated actions which demonstrate something of the will and work of the Spirit? Men from the vast world of Christianity have contributed and contribute still to peace between peoples, to the conquest of hunger and want, to the destruction of dividing barriers, to greater brotherhood on earth. The Spirit chooses people from many different nationalities and Christian groups; this is a call to ecumenical unity we cannot ignore: 'There is a variety of gifts but always the same Spirit' (1 Co 12:4).

The saying that 'the Spirit breatheth where he will' (Jn 3:8, Douay) is true. To our amazement we are hearing or experiencing for ourselves a Pentecost movement both in the Church and on its fringe and even outside it altogether. Men find themselves together at prayer, full of longing and faith that the Spirit will reveal and communicate himself to them. Individuals are grasped by his power, begin to speak of it, to talk of their conversion, to enkindle enthusiasm in others. Things that are related of the early Church and often somewhat sceptically referred to as primitive phenomena

82

suitable for beginners suddenly begin to happen again: glossolalia, prophecy, inexplicable cures. Perhaps we are equally sceptical about these modern manifestations of the Spirit. We certainly have the right to apply that ancient criterion: 'The tree can be told by its fruit' (Mt 12:33). But Paul's remarks about the Christian gatherings in Corinth must also be given their full weight: 'If you were all prophesying and an unbeliever or uninitiated person came in, he would find himself analysed and judged by everyone speaking; he would find his secret thoughts laid bare, and then fall on his face and worship God, declaring that God is among you indeed' (1 Co 14:24–25). The Spirit breathes where he will. So there are 'Whitsuns' today, too, movements sparked off by God's Spirit, or individual gestures flashing up here and there as signs of God's presence in our time. Are institutions and established churches hindrances to the working of the Spirit? Not a few Christians seem to think so. Of course there are distressing experiences which influence people to opt out or form underground churches. But God's Spirit wants to build the community up as his temple (1 Co 3:16–17), and he can burst institutions open and make use of them. Surely Vatican II's opening-up to the world was a Pentecost event, and a General Synod of Bishops could be equally so. We should not stifle the Spirit or seek to arrest the powerful movement of his coming or channel his action into outworn grooves. One may, of course, resist the promptings of the divine Spirit, as Stephen reproached the Jewish leaders with doing: 'You stubborn people, with your pagan hearts and pagan ears. You are always resisting the Holy Spirit, just as your ancestors used to do' (Ac 7:51). The Spirit who keeps renewing the world (Ps 104:30) will create new forms for himself, and who are we to impede his action?

'What must we do, brothers?' asked Peter's listeners at the first Pentecost. We too must listen to what the Spirit is saying whenever he speaks to the community. Any thought, if it leads to a common action for good, to an improvement in social conditions, to Christian unity, can be prompted by the Spirit of God. 'Hold on to what is good' (1 Th 5:21). We must be open to the promptings of the Spirit. Prayer and patience are needed, but so too is a readiness not to miss the opportunity when the Spirit calls us.

What the Spirit wants to overcome in us is apathy and discouragement. The media are happy to publish statistics of falling numbers of churchgoers and increasing numbers of defections, controversies and protests; but they are less prepared to report commitment, spontaneous gestures of assistance and the positive work of youth. They report a youth Mass in a Roman church: pop-singing, rapt attention, intercessions, a collection for poor workers, the common meal at the Lord's Table, and the fanatic who called them all 'communists' at the top of his voice; but these are just externals. Sensitivity and change of heart are not newsworthy.

At the first Christian Pentecost, the Holy Spirit chose a small group and set them on fire, and from that came a huge movement in which at least a few will never let the Spirit of Jesus go unheard. Today as always the Spirit refuses to submit to statistics and prognoses. His people are not time-servers and critical doubters, but those who open themselves to be grasped by his power and moved by his heartwarming breath.

The Church as the Fruit of the Spirit—
A Sermon for a Synod

Jn 15: 26–27; 16: 1–4 and 12–13

When the Advocate comes,
whom I shall send to you from the Father,
the Spirit of truth who issues from the Father,
he will be my witness.
And you too will be witnesses,
because you have been with me from the outset.
I have told you all this
so that your faith may not be shaken.
They will expel you from the synagogues,
and indeed the hour is coming
when anyone who kills you will think he is doing
*   a holy duty for God.*
They will do these things
because they have never known either the Father
*   or myself.*
But I have told you this,
so that when the time for it comes
you may remember that I told you.
I still have many things to say to you
but they would be too much for you now.

But when the Spirit of truth comes
he will lead you to the complete truth,
since he will not be speaking as from himself
but will say only what he has learnt;
and he will tell you of the things to come.

If we look at the Church as most people look at it today, we are hardly inclined to regard it as the fruit of the
Spirit. There is too much about it that calls for our
criticism, and its popular image is often more human
than divine. Spirit means life, movement, growth,
whereas our Church is more like a dead, crumbling
structure propped up with a few odd timbers in a half-
hearted attempt to save it from total collapse.

Can this ancient edifice be modernised, adapted to
present-day needs? Has it ceased to be what Ephesians
calls a house 'being built ... where God lives, in the
Spirit'? (2:22). I do not propose to launch into criticism
of the Church, or begin an attack on its institutional
inertia and all its cumbersome trappings. Criticism like
this was offered extremely early on, at the very beginning of the Church's life, in fact. I am thinking of the
seven circulars in the Book of Revelation which end
with: 'If anyone has ears to hear, let him listen to what
the Spirit is saying to the Churches' (2:7 and 11 etc.).
The Holy Spirit himself performs this function of
ecclesial criticism: he judges the state of the community
and its conduct, lays blame where it is due, reminds the
community of its calling and its purpose, and also, of
course, bestows praise and encouragement. This work
of the Spirit, once carried out through the preaching of
the prophets, is the theme of our reflections today. To

call the Church the fruit of the Spirit does not, of course, mean that the Church grew out of the power of the Spirit like a ripe fruit and from then on enjoys its mature bloom. We are saying that it must continually grow out of the Spirit, and that in the growing all its members are called to be uncompromisingly open to his influence.

We may begin our meditation with the words from John's Gospel we started the chapter with.

This whole Paraclete passage starts with the witness he bears to Jesus and the witness of the disciples. If the disciples' witness is named in the same breath as the Spirit's, it means that the Spirit bears witness through the disciples because he lives and works in them. And what Jesus told his disciples who had been with him from the beginning goes for us too, because we have to take over the testimony of those first witnesses and carry it on. The Johannine school in particular was convinced that the Spirit was operative in all believers. Thus John writes, for example, in his first letter: 'You have been anointed by the Holy One, and have all received the knowledge ... You have not lost the anointing that he gave you, and you do not need anyone to teach you; the anointing he gave teaches you everything; you are anointed with truth, not with a lie' (2:20 and 27). In the context John is obviously talking about true Christian belief and the need to guard against dangerous errors. We immediately ask what this means for us in our situation.

In my opinion it means that the Church shows it is the fruit of the Spirit by holding fast to the Gospel of Jesus Christ and witnessing to it in our time. In all the criticism of the institutional Church this must not be overlooked. This is its principal mission, and despite all its weaknesses and all its failures it is moved by the Spirit to testify to Jesus Christ and his message of salvation.

I can remember an extremely acid discussion once on the radio. A female student said that the Church must be dissolved because it did not tell the truth about Jesus of Nazareth. A Protestant professor, well-known for his outspoken criticisms of Christianity today, replied that he didn't agree. If the Churches disappeared, he said, it would not be long before all knowledge of Jesus and what he stood for were lost to the world. For better or for worse, the Churches have handed on all we know of Jesus and his message, even when it stands against them as their accuser. In fact there are plenty of examples from Church history.

The Spirit who reminds the Church of Jesus's words and deeds also forces it constantly to re-examine itself in the light of the Gospel and to stand at the judgement seat of Jesus's word. What we see happening in the Church today seems to me to be a dose of salts from God's Spirit. He blows like a powerful wind and sweeps away all the chaff. In today's society with its irritating but salutary urge for information and publicity, he makes it impossible for the Church to hide its weaknesses and faults, or rest satisfied with soothing words. The Gospel said this a long time ago: 'Whatever you have said in the dark will be heard in the daylight, and what you have whispered in hidden places will be proclaimed on the housetops' (Lk 12 : 3). Is the Spirit of God not to make use of public media to cleanse the Church of its stains and creases? But let us not leave this job to others, but ourselves admit what is evil and rotten so that the true witness of our faith may then be heard again.

It is up to us to let the Spirit work through us wherever there is a need for fearless witness against the trends of the times and human pleasure-seeking. In our Gospel passage, we are told about the world's hostility and the invective and ill-treatment Christ's witnesses can expect. If we lack the courage to oppose the opinions of many of our contemporaries, we betray the Gospel. I am thinking of particular moral questions—the institution of marriage, education and the like—but also of the profounder understanding of human existence about which Jesus said: 'What gain ... is it for a man to win the whole world and ruin his life?' (Mk 8 : 36).

Naturally we all regret that not everybody in the Church today is of one mind on all issues; but mostly it is a question not of denying the faith altogether, but of working out its implications differently and understanding it in practice. Our passage from John has something pertinent to say on this too: 'I still have many things to say to you but they would be too much for you now. But when the Spirit of truth comes he will lead you to the complete truth' (16:12–13). Jesus is aware of the difficulties his disciples will come up against and he knows their weak points; so he sends them his Spirit who is to lead them to the complete truth. Hence what we know as the first Pentecost; the Church came into being as the fruit of the Spirit. But even after Pentecost, the Church consists of men who must struggle for a knowledge of the truth and right-doing, and find it hard to make the proper decisions for the future. We are experiencing this in the work of the

Synod. Men who profess the same faith and each in his own way stand for the things that are Christ's take different views on many issues. We all want the best for the Church; but we have to realise that in many matters reliance on one's own thinking, on lengthy argument and debate are futile; we must put all our confidence in the Holy Spirit who leads us to the complete truth.

The Church, the community of those who believe in Jesus Christ, is for ever new because it is the fruit of the Spirit. Ignatius of Antioch, that great bishop and martyr of a sub-apostolic times, once remarked: 'Christianity is not a matter of persuasion, but a work of the Power' (Letter to the Romans 3:3). It is not the most important thing for us to strive for sublime thoughts to commit them to paper. Rather we must be a witness that it is the Spirit of Jesus who moves us, that he unites us and guides our deliberations. Let us pray that this Spirit who creates new life may be with us now and grant his strength to overcome our weakness!

Out of Darkness into Light

Col 1: 12–13

*[Thank] the Father who has made it possible for you
to join the saints and with them to inherit the light.
Because that is what he has done: he has taken us out
of the power of darkness and created a place for us in
the kingdom of the Son that he loves.*

We have here a biblical image describing the Gentiles'
entry into salvation when they accept the Christian
faith. Behind it we see a reference to baptism which
was frequently regarded in the early Church as an entry
into the kingdom of God's light. So for example we
read in Ephesians: 'You were darkness once, but now
you are light in the Lord' (5:8). And in Peter's first
letter, the Gentile Christians are called on to 'sing the
praises of God who called you out of darkness into his
wonderful light' (2:9). Similarly here the Colossians are
urged to thank the Father with joy who has snatched
them from the power of darkness and given them a
place in the kingdom of his beloved Son.

The 'darkness' is not so much distance from God, or the darkness of uncertainty as to what constitutes human salvation, or even the night and poverty of a life spent in sin and vice. It is more than that: it is a force grasping for control of man, a 'power' out to overcome him and do him violence. From man's point of view it could be described as being caught up in a situation in which evil is unavoidable. No person is certain not to succumb to his own proclivity to evil, or not to become a sacrifice to iniquity and violence. Behind the desperation and estrangement of man's earthly, historical situation, the Bible sees the work of God's Adversary. Even if we ignore all the mythical, magical and human pictures of the 'Devil', the 'Prince of this world', we are still left with the fact that the world as we experience it is full of lies and murder, hate and greed, the lust for power and unbridled passion. What it is exactly to which we attribute this concentration of evil, this unimaginable mass of affliction in history and in our own present is less important. The fact itself is there beyond doubt for all to see, and stands as a warning against over-optimistic prognoses of the future. Faith speaks of a 'mysterium iniquitatis', a mystery of evil.

God the Father who is light and love has snatched us from the power of darkness; he has made it possible for us 'to join the saints and with them to inherit the light'. This is a remarkable phrase; we have gained a better understanding of its meaning since the discovery of the Qumran texts. The 'saints' there are the angels who dwell with God and surround his throne in the world of light. We all hope to be united with these 'sons of heaven' and to share in their 'inheritance'. There is another image : a heavenly banquet, but it attests equally to the reality of God and his world. It is not, of course, a world like ours, a higher storey of the cosmic edifice, but a 'heaven above the heavens', a transcendent world far beyond the capacities of human representation. It is transcendent not because it exceeds the extent of the universe, but because it surpasses the limits of human experience. Distant and yet near at hand, without any spatial texture, this is a spiritual kingdom in which God is disclosed. One can also talk about this transcendence as the depth-dimension of human existence, the Ground towards which man is driven by his thirst for the Absolute.

This world of God's is Christ's kingdom in which we are given a place. The Father bestowed dominion and power on his beloved Son when he raised him from the dead and set him at his right hand (cf. Ep 1 : 20–21). What does this mean if not that Christ is now God's Envoy who destroys evil by wresting us from the 'power of darkness' and creating a place for us in the kingdom 'of the light'? It is through Christ that even while we sojourn in this earthly, visible world, a new, hidden world, the bright world of God's grace, is opened up for us. We are not carried off out of the darkness here below into a higher kingdom of light, but drawn by Christ into the sphere of God's life and placed under his dominion, which even now brings with it into our earthly existence light and transparence, peace and joy.

Christ's kingdom has nothing of the earthly or tangible, nothing of the historically experiential about it, nor is it the Church in its visible realisation. It is rather God's world revealed by faith to which we belong in

Christ as members of the Church which is his Body. It is a world in which all earthly darkness is swallowed up in light, in which the love of God's beloved Son reigns supreme, and the life of the Risen Christ conquers death.

Even so this kingdom is not a paradise to which we rise to rest and forget the troubles of this life. We are still citizens of the earth, and as such have to prove ourselves worthy of our heavenly calling and domicile. The promise that we are 'light in the Lord' is immediately followed in Ephesians by a caution: 'Be like children of light ... Try to discover what the Lord wants of you, having nothing to do with the futile works of darkness' (5:8–11). For these Christian converts from paganism, baptism meant not only entry into the kingdom of God's light, but also a very strict obligation to renounce the old life of sin and vice, and a constant determination to surrender daily to the lordship of Christ. At the same time the awareness of belonging to his kingdom gave them calm, confidence, and an inner peace. Paul refers to this Christian experience when he writes in Romans: 'If you have hope, this will make you cheerful. Do not give up if trials come; and keep on praying' (12:12).

Is this kingdom of Christ a dream and a delusion? No, it is the dimension of redeemed existence which unfolds to the person who believes. The crucified Jesus lives and reigns. Where Christ is with his Spirit, his power and his love, there is his kingdom.

The Mystery of Christ

Col 1: 26–27

God's message to you ... was a mystery hidden for generations and centuries and has now been revealed to his saints. It was God's purpose to reveal it to them and to show all the rich glory of this mystery to pagans.

This text, in which Paul impresses on the Gentile Christians at Colossae the greatness of their faith as Christians, speaks of a mystery hidden for generations but now revealed. What sort of mystery is it? The reference to 'Christ among you' is a first word of explanation: the mystery of God is based on the person of Christ and concerns his significance for all peoples. It is not a truth kept secret up till then and still unknown, but a reality suddenly made manifest. As Paul later says, the mystery of God is Christ in whom 'all the jewels of wisdom and knowledge are hidden' (2:2), or the 'mystery of Christ' as it is called towards the end of the same letter (4:3). Does Paul mean that all secrets are revealed in Christ and all riddles answered? No; he

95

speaks of one mystery only, but one which is of unsuspected depth and significance.

If we wish to gain greater insight into this 'mystery of Christ', it is helpful to turn to an earlier Pauline text, 1 Co 2:6–10. Here he is talking about God's 'foolishness' and wisdom. 'The hidden wisdom of God which we teach in our mysteries is the wisdom that God predestined to be for our glory before the ages began' (v. 7). In the context it is obvious what is referred to as divine 'foolishness' (1:25), which for the Christian believers is the divine 'wisdom': it is the Cross of Jesus Christ through which God has willed to save those who have faith when human wisdom had failed to know God (1:21). Behind the dark event of the crucifixion, Paul sees the 'Rulers of this Age'—the spiritual powers which in his view are the real actors in the world's unfolding drama, or their human satellites, the political rulers who put Jesus to death. But these evil regents have not known God's wisdom; otherwise they would not have crucified the 'Lord of Glory' (2:8). For the crucified Jesus did not remain in death; he was raised by God and exalted. Those who intended to destroy the Redeemer in fact brought about his Lordship; when he became man's Saviour he broke their power. This is the paradox of God's ways, of his wisdom that was hidden but is now revealed. However strange and mythical these 'powers' seem to us today, the thought behind them is quite clear: in God's wisdom, the Cross of Jesus becomes the source of salvation.

In our passage from Colossians, the emphasis is not on the defeat of the evil powers, but on the mediation of salvation in all its abundance. This reveals another dimension of the divine mystery: salvation has been brought to all peoples the world over, and the Colossians too are invited to share in it. What is meant by 'the rich glory' of the mystery? It is a characteristic conception of this letter that we have already been raised up with Christ (2:12) and our life is now hidden with him in God (3:3). Freed from sin and guilt (2:13), we are raised up to God, and with Christ triumph over the Sovereignties and Powers (cf. 2:14-15). This gives our hope supreme certainty: through sharing in Christ's Cross and resurrection we are already embraced by his glory in which we too shall be revealed when Christ is revealed (3:4).

These are lofty thoughts in lofty language. We sense something of the writer's irresistible excitement and the enthusiasm he is trying to arouse in the converted Gentiles. We have become very unsentimental; but it is still worth our while to ponder the 'mystery of Christ' which those Christians had experienced with such joy. 'Christ among you, your hope of glory': Christ is a living reality for the believer which permeates and stamps his life. In Galatians Paul writes: 'I live now not with my own life but with the life of Christ who lives in me', and he continues: 'The life I now live in this body I live in faith: faith in the Son of God who loved me and who sacrificed himself for my sake' (2:20). Earthly life has a new content, a deeper meaning and destination. Grasped by the love of Christ, it has become a life spent in the service of his Lord who is both heavenly and yet close to the believer and inwardly present to him. We catch a glimpse from the apostle's letters of how much his life must have been lived out under the mystery of Christ. It is very far from being a flight from the world or a piece of fanaticism; in his total devotion to Christ, this missionary preacher of the early Church intends to prove himself a servant of God 'by great fortitude in times of suffering; in times of hardship and distress ...' (2 Co 6:4–6). The Christian life is indeed a daily dying (1 Co 15:31), a surrender to death for Jesus's sake in which Jesus's life is openly shown in our mortal flesh (2 Co 4:11). This life, however, is borne up by an inner strength which flows from the crucified and risen Lord; it is filled out with an inner glory which comes from hope.

Christ is our 'hope in glory'. The darkness of earthly existence, which surrounds the believer like anybody else, lights up for him in his hope for the future that God has revealed to him. God's pledge is Christ, crucified and risen. The living Christ who dwells with God is the mystery of God in whom our future is secured.

Hidden Glory

Col 3: 3–4

You have died, and now the life you have is hidden with Christ in God. But when Christ is revealed—and he is your life—you too will be revealed in all your glory with him.

This is a text which expresses our hope more concisely and forcefully than almost any other in the New Testament. From their baptism onwards when the Gentile converts 'died with Christ to the principles of this word' (2:20), when in other words they were freed from slavery to all oppressive forces, from the compulsion of fate, from subjection to what is merely worldly and transitory, from sin and guilt, they are men of hope. For the Christian, life is no longer limited by death: it is filled with a new hope-giving life.

The 'life' referred to in this context is not the tangible, worldly, historical life that runs its course between birth and death. But then it is not totally alien to and distant from that either. Man takes a step towards it when he strives for ultimate, perfect, lasting self-fulfilment, which he cannot despite all his own efforts reach. Is there such a life? Faith answers that such a life is imparted to us when we are brought to 'true life with Christ' (3:1). The life of the risen Christ is already ours, only we do not yet possess it openly, in direct experience and happiness. But it is important to the writer of Colossians (Paul or a disciple who shares his theology) that we do not have to wait for this life until after we are dead. No, it has been implanted already in our earthly existence, it is already present and active in us.

Can we experience this life in any way? Paul is convinced that we can, and he says so on numerous occasions. He mentions it, for example, when he says that our 'inner man' is renewed day by day if we look to what is invisible; what is visible soon passes, but what is invisible remains forever (2 Co 4:17–18). He experiences Christ's strength in his own weakness (cf. 2 Co 12:9–10); he knows he is weak with the crucified Jesus, but also strong with Christ who 'lives now through the power of God' (2 Co 13:4). The life of Christ is given him in the Holy Spirit whose reality and effectiveness also can be lived and experienced. Paul is relying on his experiences at prayer when he writes: 'The Spirit himself and our spirit bear united witness that we are children of God' (Rm 8:16). He is convinced that all Christians can have experiences like his because the Spirit reveals himself. He does so not only in extraordinary external charisms (cf. 1 Co 12–14), but also in the Christian's day to day living. God's Spirit leads us to do good (Ga 5:16; Rm 8:13), and bears spiritual fruit in us (Ga 5:22). So the life of the Spirit who lives in us

100

can be experienced at least in its effects.

At the moment, however, we live 'by faith and not by sight' (2 Co 5:7). In our passage from Colossians, we are told that our life 'is hidden with Christ in God'. The meaning is the same. Following the world-views of the time, the image is a spatial one: Christ is 'above' in God, and we should be directing our thoughts and our efforts there (3:2). But the thought is not necessarily tied to spatial categories. 'In God' is an expression for God's present dominion and glory which is hidden in the world as we experience it, but which is also the most fundamental reality supporting everything and the goal towards which everything strives. The risen Christ lives 'in God', which is to say that he has reached the goal. To the extent that we live with and in Christ, we too have entered God's life. This life is still hidden, but it is safe in God.

In due course, when Christ 'our life' appears, this hiddenness will be all light and transparence. The 'parousia' or second coming of Christ is often thought of as an event of the last days. But here it is not seen as a cosmic event or dramatic happening relegated to the end of time; it is the completion of our Christian existence. The question of its how and when is therefore irrelevant. The Christian's gaze is totally on what he will become. The hidden glory of the life which is already ours will be revealed to us. Then we ourselves shall achieve the transfiguration which in Jesus's resurrection has made his crucified body glorious (Ph 3:21).

'Christ our life' has a mystical ring about it, but the reference is not so much to a mystical experience as to a whole existence lived and mastered in faith. From his prison Paul writes to the Philippian Christians: 'I know this will help to save me, thanks to your prayers and to the help which will be given to me by the Spirit of Jesus. My one hope and trust is that I shall never have to admit defeat, but that now as always I shall have the courage for Christ to be glorified in my body, whether by my life or by my death. Life to me, of course, is Christ' (Ph 1 : 19–21). For Paul earthly life has gained a fresh dimension: it is filled with Christ. This does not mean merely that his thoughts are governed by what is Christ's; much more than that, it means that Christ has become a living reality to him which he experiences in himself. Only this can explain his subsequent wish to die and be totally with Christ (vv. 21–24).

Not all Christians, perhaps only a few, experience 'Christ in us' as a reality with the same personal certainty as Paul did. Perhaps a certainty like his comes only in the frontier situations of life, when we are in extreme danger or face to face with death. Yet we can still say that Christ is our life because we believe that we have a share in his Cross and Resurrection.

Because Christ is our life in this sense, our hope has an unshakeable basis. 'When we were reconciled to God by the death of his Son, we were still enemies; now that we have been reconciled, surely we may count on being saved by the life of his Son?' (Rm 5 : 10). Only then will everything that we have borne concealed in our lives be revealed. Christ's life will be revealed in us in all its glory.

God's Love—Our Hope in This Vale of Tears

Rm 8: 35-39

Nothing therefore can come between us and the love of Christ, even if we are troubled or worried, or being persecuted, or lacking food or clothes, or being threatened or even attacked. As scripture promised: 'For your sake we are being massacred daily, and reckoned as sheep for the slaughter.' These are the trials through which we triumph, by the power of him who loved us.

For I am certain of this: neither death nor life, no angel, no prince, nothing that exists, nothing still to come, not any power, or height or depth, nor any created thing, can ever come between us and the love of God made visible in Christ Jesus our Lord.

This section is the climax and conclusion of Paul's long and animated reflection on the Christian in the world. After a number of interruptions and theological excursions, in chapter 8 he resumes the line of thought he originally formulated briefly in chapter 5: in Jesus

Christ we have gained salvation, we have found peace with God, and yet we are still subject to the hardships and pressures of this life. Even these, though, contribute to our salvation, because they provide constant trials to strengthen our hope, which is a hope that is not deceptive because the love of God has been poured into our hearts by the Holy Spirit. Such compact thoughts as these scarcely begin to explain the stress of our earthly situation in the firm hope of salvation (for example, Paul says very little about the misery of this life beyond referring to its 'sufferings'), and therefore needed to be explained more fully. Paul would not be the man and theologian we know him to be, eager and restless, if he did not go on to enumerate all the external and internal troubles of human existence and then *still*, all the more passionately, profess his belief and his indestructible hope in man's redemption.

In chapter 8, he first talks about the 'sufferings' of this life in v. 18, but they are drowned in the increasingly jubilant expectation of salvation: 'I think that what we suffer in this life can never be compared to the glory, as yet unrevealed, which is waiting for us.' But then he reflects on the unsolved difficulties of the created and historical world in a melancholy language which quite captures the pessimistic mood of contemporary Jewish apocalyptic. We are told about creation's inward groaning for the revelation of the Son of God; creation is caught up in slavery to decadence, and can be set free only when the freedom of the children of God takes place in all its glory. All creation has been groaning as if in the pangs of childbirth (vv. 19–22 NEB). In the course of this gloomy description, Paul now speaks about the groaning of those who already possess the 'first-fruits of the Spirit': they too groan for their bodies to be set free. Then he adds that our awaited redemption has not yet overcome all the difficulties of our existence, that this world of ours is still full of suffering and pain, even for those who believe in salvation through Jesus Christ.

We have to be grateful to Paul for not glossing over the problem of suffering in the world. For many today it is the abyss in which all aspirations ultimately shatter. The pain of the innocent creature, indescribable pain in which millions of guiltless men are swallowed up daily, seems to be the pitiless contradiction of a merciful God, the proof of the absurdity of all that happens on earth. 'Last of all the God of Christians died in Auschwitz.' But then he had been dead already for over nineteen hundred years—on the Cross with the superscription 'Jesus of Nazareth King of the Jews'.

Paul too suffers, he too groans with the rest of creation. After that gloomy picture, only slowly does he come round to speaking of the hope in invisible things, of the constancy which must go with the expectation (vv. 24–25). The Spirit of God takes on our weakness and expresses our plea in a way that could never be put into words, he himself groans in and with us. Such sighs do not go unheeded or misunderstood at the throne of God (vv. 26–27). It is a singular view intelligible only in its proper context and before the backdrop of a profound experience of prayer.

Then Paul takes courage and expresses a tremendous confidence: 'We know that to those who love God everything conspires for good,' or as we can also translate it, 'we know that by turning everything to their good God co-operates with all those who love him'

105

(v. 28). But it is only when he looks to Jesus Christ that the apostle achieves his total certainty. Jesus Christ is the image of redeemed man's goal; he is the 'eldest of many brothers' (v. 29). There is no doubt that Paul is thinking of the risen Christ who by his Cross has conquered all darkness and pain. In him God has opted for us (v. 31), and given an answer to the ever-nagging question of suffering and death: he did not spare his own Son, but gave him up to benefit us all (v. 32). With him he has given us his all. Even if the question Why is without a rational answer, for the believer one thing is certain: God gave a concrete answer in the resurrection of his crucified Son. So finally the apostle's hope turns totally to Jesus Christ: he is our surety and advocate, the dead and risen Jesus who now stands and pleads for us at God's right hand (v. 34).

Thus Paul has again progressed from the misery of the present earthly existence, from the anxious question of human suffering scarcely articulated except through groans, to the hope of faith. Now he can stare all pain and the horror of death squarely in the eye, and with bold, indeed jubilant and indomitable courage, he can exclaim: 'Nothing ... can come between us and the love of Christ' (v. 35). He follows this with a list of human afflictions and sufferings which burden our present death-marked existence, and which are summed up in a verse from the Psalms: 'For your sake we are being massacred daily, and reckoned as sheep for the slaughter' (Ps 44:11). All this, though, no longer frightens him: we triumph in the end, absolutely certain that we need not fear even the superhuman powers. Paul enumerates these in the understanding and terminology of his time, but with the last one ('nor any created thing') he expresses his conviction that after all it is only transitory, inferior, dependent powers who oppose the Creator of all, and he will not relinquish his control of the universe.

But no meditation on the world and its history, only contemplating the event that was Jesus Christ, can lead Paul to the invincible optimism he expresses. In Jesus God has revealed his hidden love, despite all appearances to the contrary, although it remains hidden for those who look on him with unseeing eyes. But the person who believes understands that God has irrevocably promised us and shared with us his love in Jesus Christ. Only this love of God's of which in Jesus Christ we are now certain, can sustain us in the abyss of pain, through all our anxious questioning, and in this vale of tears give us everlasting hope.

The Light of Hope—A Meditation for Committed Christians

1 Jn 2: 7–10

My dear people,
this is not a new commandment that I am writing
    to tell you,
but an old commandment
that you were given from the beginning,
the original commandment which was the mess-
    age brought to you.
Yet in another way, what I am writing to you,
and what is being carried out in your lives as it
    was in his,
is a new commandment;
because the night is over
and the real light is already shining.
Anyone who claims to be in the light
but hates his brother
is still in the dark.
But anyone who loves his brother is living in the
    light
and need not be afraid of stumbling.

The Spanish philosopher Miguel Unamuno once said:
'If you want to know what a person believes, you must
ask him what he hopes for.' But today there are people
who have even given up hope. This is shocking, because
it is against human nature. Bertolt Brecht confesses: 'I
have no hope. Only the blind speak of a way out
whereas I can see. When even mistakes have worn thin,
one's last companion is always Nothing.' This is naked
nihilism; but can a man live with it? According to
Albert Camus, progress, true freedom, includes the re-
nunciation of all hope: 'The sole freedom I know is
that of thought and action. Loss of hope and loss of the
future means for man an added space in which to be.
... This absurd world without God is now being
peopled with men who think clearly and hope no
more.' To my mind these men Camus speaks of are not
really men at all, but ice-cold calculators, lifeless
robots, potential suicides.

Where there is no hope we get darkness, cold and
stiffness—in a word, death. Life is movement towards a
goal; it is always shaping itself with an eye to the future,
and in doing so finds strength to face the present.
Human life means grasping for the future with one's
reason and will, it means planning and trusting that the
plans will mature—in short it means hoping. We can
understand the frightful aberration of a philosophy of
despair only as a product of the unfathomable disillu-
sion into which the state of our world has brought so
many people. This is an indictment of the whole of
humanity, and of Christianity in particular. We must
consider where our fault lies and where we can remedy
it. We may not speak too quickly of our hope. Only if
we feel something of the world's darkness and chill,

something of so many people's despair and yet can still hope, will our hope not degenerate into more despair.

In Johannine theology, darkness is seen as the kingdom of the forces opposed to God, in contrast with the kingdom of light, which is God's world. It is a sinister, aggressive power clutching at men and tumbling them in despair to destruction. 'Walk while you have the light, or the dark will overtake you; he who walks in the dark does not know where he is going' (Jn 12:35). The first letter of John shares this background of dualistic thinking with the Gospel. Christian hope seems to break through even more dazzlingly, for example in the reading we have taken as our text: 'The real light is already shining.' But the tone of the letter is basically one of admonition, and the hope is pretty forcefully coupled with the Christian responsibility to exercise practical brotherly love. This is the only way to make faith credible and hope convincing. Otherwise all one's verbal protestations are so much whitewash, and like the Gnostic heretics whom the writer reproaches for despising brotherly love, one sinks more and more deeply into the blinding darkness.

We are told of a commandment that is both old and new: old because we were given it from the beginning, new because it makes all things new and banishes the night. John is addressing Christians who have lived for quite some time in a Christian community. They have got over the novelty of their new-found Christianity and the fervour of their first enthusiasm; they live in an established Christian milieu. But the old message must be constantly brought home to them in its never-ageing freshness. Their situation, then, is like ours. In the

110

community John is writing to, certain members of it are confusing the faithful with ideas and talk which are at variance with the essence of the Christian faith and its moral demands. The writer counters by pointing out that one cannot have God without accepting Christ who came in the flesh, and one cannot accept Jesus Christ without putting his crucial demand of love into practice. 'The old commandment is the message brought to you.' From other passages in the letter, it is clear that this message brought to us in the beginning is the law of love which Jesus himself laid down. 'We [must] love one another as he told us to' (3 : 23). It is very noticeable how this letter with its heightened Christology always goes back to the historical Jesus. His example too is involved: 'We are in God only when the one who claims to be living in him is living the same kind of life as Christ lived' (2 : 6).

Jesus was a light in the world's darkness. With his knowledge of God he taught men true humanity, and showed them how the world can be different. He gave his disciples a single commandment with enough substance in it to provide a whole life's programme, a commandment which was not entirely new but which in him took on newness. In our reading, this is expressed as follows: this new commandment 'is being carried out in your lives as it was in his', so it is not just a bit of wishful thinking or a piece of pious advice, but a concrete reality. The writer is obviously thinking of Jesus's commitment even to the point of death, which in his eyes was not just a past event, but a permanent revelation and the permanent guarantee of God's love for us. With his living and dying Jesus gave love room to spread in, and we can again move freely and step with hope into the future. The night is over, and the real light is already shining.

But let us not overlook the first part of the phrase: this new commandment is being carried out 'in *your* lives'. The space *Jesus* opened up for love is for *us* to enter, too. The writer is so convinced of the genuine Christian conduct of the community that he speaks without hesitation of the reality of their brotherly love. Elsewhere he says: 'We have passed out of death and into life, and of this we can be sure because we love our brothers' (3 : 14). Brotherly love is the sign of sonship of God. This doesn't mean that the writer thinks the love present in the community is already perfect. We must not forget some very serious cautions: 'This has taught us love—that he gave up his life for us; and we, too, ought to give up our lives for our brothers,' and John follows this immediately with a daily Christian responsibility: 'If a man who was rich enough in this world's goods saw that one of his brothers was in need, but closed his heart to him, how could the love of God be living in him? My children, our love is not to be just words or mere talk, but something real and active' (3 : 16–18).

So we are not to rely on high-flown words, but must get on with what we can do. We cannot hope to conquer all suffering, all injustice or all need in the world; but like the earthly Jesus we can, with our personal commitment, our assistance to those in need around us, our almsgiving, give some signs of our love. This certainly is not all we are called on to do. Today we have to use all our social and political influence to help underprivileged and oppressed groups and peoples. It is up to us to animate and activate the whole Church in this direction. But however necessary criticism and con-science-stirrings, appeals and actions are in public, there is still the appeal to our hearts not to shut our-selves off from our brothers in their time of need.

The real light is already shining. But if it has to be a light of hope for the men of our time, Christ's love must be seen to be real in us. 'Anyone who claims to be in the light but hates his brother is still in the dark. But anyone who loves his brother is living in the light.' In this light we, too, even in our time, can step confidently into the future.

Who is Jesus of Nazareth—for Me?
A Personal Profession of Faith

I have always been struck by the way the disciples left their jobs and followed Jesus. What drove these men with families and trades to join Jesus of Nazareth, to share the rigours of his wandering life, to remain with him even when opposition grew and the hostility of the authorities became increasingly obvious? Jesus did not call them to join a political liberation front, he did not announce a programme of social revolution. But what he brought was a message that touches every man's heart most intimately: the message of God who wills man's happiness, peace and salvation.

Jesus's invitation to discipleship is unique: it is not like taking on pupils, opening up a club or recruiting an army. It is an invitation to personal companionship with Jesus, a call to travel the same road with him, to work at a service of man which he himself above all others has worked at already. It is this call to discipleship that, for me at any rate, best displays Jesus's authority which with all its greatness and power to command, still leaves man utterly free, and indeed gives him a new freedom. An absolute claim, an unerring sense of authority, a hidden mystery: it is these things that prove Jesus's total intimacy with God. I have not difficulty in explaining the inner mystery of this man Jesus, who can become every man's guide and fellow-traveller, by qualifying him with the title 'Son of God'. For me Jesus is the unique revelation of God in his address to man and claim on man, such as there never was before him or will be after, and I feel that this call and claim are made on me personally.

John's Gospel, which has particularly occupied my thoughts in my theological work, clarifies for me in a particular way, which is at once time-conditioned and yet timeless, the unique significance of the person of Jesus for myself and for everyone. A lot would have to be said and clarified if I were not to be misunderstood. But I want just to take one sentence which I find particularly illuminating on the question of discipleship: 'I am the light of the world; anyone who follows me will not be walking in the dark; he will have the light of life' (8:12). This is not a magic Gnostic formula explaining human existence in mythical language, or a call to self-discovery, but an invitation to follow Jesus. Here again the earthly Jesus is prominent with his road to death on the Cross and his commandment to love which sums up everything that is demanded of me. But it has become a saying of the living, ever-present Lord who promises the light of life to whoever believes.

As a young man I determined to accept this invitation of Jesus to be his disciple because it seemed to me to be the greatest thing I could live for. From that moment, despite all the historical changes and spiritual vicissitudes of my generation, I have not been mistaken. Indeed, all these upheavals, the sheer 'historicity' of everything human, the transitoriness of human

115

ideologies, the short-lived vogue of even the most passionate popular movements have only led me to adhere more closely still to Jesus of Nazareth. He shows me what is most deeply human, the needs common to all men in their humanity, and the longing for the ultimate fulfilment of their being which cannot be stifled or silenced with material things. His life and work in history are programmatic and exemplary: a herald of limitless love and an advocate for the poor and despised, a helper of the weak, a man of understanding and forgiveness to sinners, a harsh critic of stony-hearted men who misuse their position, wealth and power, their intellectual and spiritual authority, a man quick to detect untruthfulness and hypocrisy, a man of God for whom only God's standards are good enough: God is no respecter of persons, he looks not to what is exterior but to man's heart.

Even Jesus's life on earth seems to me exemplary: people's favour, the judgement of men, is irresolute and unreliable, success and external happiness are but temporary. No one can escape trial, suffering and death. Jesus too had to tread this path, and he accepted it with joy. Although rejected by man, he was acknowledged by God. The man who outwardly was a failure, who was executed on a cross, is justified by God, raised up and made 'Prince of Life'. This is not a myth, but the profoundest interpretation of human existence, which in the historical Jesus becomes for those who believe truth and reality, trust and hope.

So in my discipleship of Jesus I have not been disappointed. The only thing is, in myself I still experience the feeble and paltry nature of all human endeavour, even in the service which since Jesus's call I have been determined to follow. As well as my personal failure and falling short of Jesus's demands, I have to acknowledge our limited field of vision, the narrowness of the human mind and heart, even in the community of those who are my fellow-believers in Jesus and my fellow-disciples. The massive reaction of today's youth against Christianity and the Church frightens and dismays me, although I have to admit that we have often given a false picture of Jesus's message, passed over too much of it in silence, and failed to put a lot into practice. This is especially true in the area of Christian social commitment. We have put too much emphasis on the 'Christ-cult'—the honour paid to the ever-present Lord, and consequently neglected the wishes and demands of the historical Jesus. We have paid too much attention to an individualistic sort of piety and a triumphalistic image of the Church. We have a great deal to think through again and much to learn, we theologians perhaps most of all.

Our teacher is still, as always, Jesus of Nazareth, unfathomable in his person, inexhaustible in his Gospel. We must inquire more and more deeply into the intentions of the historical Jesus, and meditate on their implications for mankind, in particular for society today. On the other hand, not a few people in our generation, even theologians, seem to me to fall into the other extreme, into one-sided views and even errors. Jesus did not advocate social reforms and structural changes exclusively or even insistently. He preached the New Man who is created in God's image, lives by his love and brings that love to men.

As Jesus's disciple, I am always a long way behind my Master; but he is still my Guide when I stray from

117

the path and my helper when I flag. So Jesus of Nazareth for me is not only a light from the past, but a present Lord who is always near and to whom I can look and pray. He is also the ground of my hope. I am certain that he will always move many hearts, including those of young people, with his message. That is my human hope for a reeling mankind dancing on the edge of the abyss. But my last hope, even if it is 'against all hope', arises from my belief that God raised the crucified Jesus from the dead.